AMERICAN
PATCHWORK
QUILTS

AMERICAN PATCHWORK QUILTS

Lenice Ingram Bacon

Photography by
Creative Photographers, Boston

BONANZA BOOKS
NEW YORK

This edition is published by Bonanza Books,
a division of Crown Publishers, Inc.,
by arrangement with William Morrow & Company, Inc.
a b c d e f g h
BONANZA 1980 EDITION

Manufactured in the United States of America

Library of Congress Cataloging in Publication Data

Bacon, Lenice Ingram.
    American patchwork quilts.

    Reprint of the ed. published by Morrow, New York.
    Bibliography: p. 185.
    Includes index.
    1. Quilting. 2. Patchwork. 3. Coverlets-
United States. I. Title.
[TT835.B23 1980]   746.46   79-27332
ISBN 0-517-30940-8

DEDICATED

to

my late husband

whose encouragement

in my many projects

was never-failing

and

to my children, who,

with loving sufferance,

have shared my interest

ACKNOWLEDGMENTS

To acknowledge all the sources of inspiration that have helped to meld this book into one piece would be extremely difficult. But to all those who have had a part in it, my deep gratitude: Annie R. Offen and Herbert Offen, loyal friends and quilt lovers; Dr. and Mrs. Gustave Laurenzi, discriminating collectors of Americana; Margaret J. Snider, Reference Librarian, Newton Free Library, Newton, Massachusetts; Sally Wells, Director of Mountain Artisans, Charleston, West Virginia; Constance McMullan of Beauport Museum, Gloucester, Massachusetts; Louise Carlisle; Jeanette Burns; Dorothy Tarwater; Rose Tedder Kidd; Grace M. Hollett; Marsha Ridder Van Vliet; Alfred Allan Lewis—to name a few.

In addition to this list of individuals, my appreciative thanks go to the following museums for their generous cooperation and assistance, especially to Larry Salmon, Curator of Textiles, Museum of Fine Arts, Boston, Massachusetts; American Museum in Britain, Claverton Manor, Bath, England, Ian McCullum, Curator and Director; Association for the Preservation of Virginia Antiquities, and photographer Ron Jennings, Virginia Museum, both in Richmond, Virginia; Cape Ann Historical Association and Museum, Caroline E. Benham, Assistant Curator; Concord Antiquarian Society, Laurence Henry, Director; Mrs. Charles A. Potter, Librarian, Essex Institute, Salem, Massachusetts; Friends of the Jackson Homestead Historical Museum, Newton, Massachusetts, Ruth G. Cannard, Director-Curator; Shelburne Museum, Inc., Shelburne, Vermont, Richard Lawrence Greene, Assistant to the Director; Wenham Historical Association and Museum, Wenham, Massachusetts, Irene Dodge, Director.

I am grateful to the early writers of books on quilts. Their contributions not only helped to keep the art of quiltmaking alive during that period when the quilt had fallen into obscurity, their research also added to the knowledge of many other phases of Americana. Marie D. Webster's *Quilts: Their Story and How to Make Them*, published in 1926—the first book that came to my attention—became a Bible for quilt lovers and researchers. Two very valuable volumes followed: Ruth E. Finley's comprehensive work, *Old Patchwork Quilts and the Women Who Made Them*, in 1929, and Florence Peto's *Historic Quilts*, in 1939. Both became authoritative sources, and it was my privilege to know personally these two dedicated writers.

And last, but by no means least, I am greatly indebted to the wise editorship and unwavering support of Sylvia Winsor Dudley, together with the unique combination of skilled guidance and inspiring warmth of Narcisse Chamberlain.

CONTENTS

LIST OF
ILLUSTRATIONS

List of Illustrations

AMERICAN
PATCHWORK
QUILTS

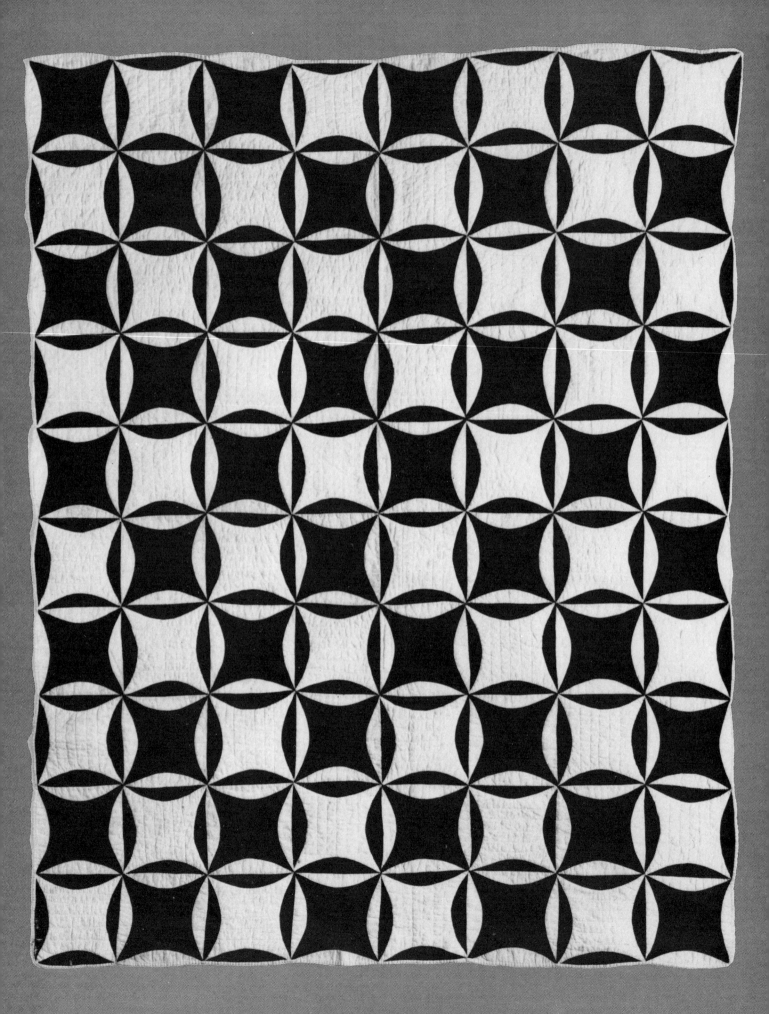

INTRODUCTION

During my years of involvement with quilts, one question has been asked so often that I have come to expect it. "How did you happen to become interested in quilts?", said with the slightly veiled innuendo of "Quilts, of all things!"

My friends who lectured on their favorite subjects —china, glass, hooked rugs, even fans—were all accepted without question. But quilts were different and my absorption in them seemed a bit queer. There were times when I threatened to get a more stylish hobby such as French snuffboxes or Chinese porcelains.

I was still a young woman when I first began lecturing and I came to realize that my audiences were surprised that I was not older. I could understand this, for until the recent revival of interest in quilts and everything connected with them, the very word evoked a picture of elderly ladies sewing and rocking peacefully in the sunshine.

It is not easy to answer the question directly. When I was a child, quilts held a sense of mystery for me,

PLATE 1

Lafayette Orange Peel. An old pattern, yet so modern in feeling. It is a difficult one for any quiltmaker, not a design for beginners. It took experience and skill to manipulate the eliptical pieces, even in the days when the ladies would undertake anything. This quilt, in dark brown and white—the brown pieces cut from a crepe material—must have been a challenge indeed. Made in orange and white, it is very effective and reminiscent of the story that has come down through the years. The Marquis de Lafayette created a stir among the guests at a banquet given in his honor during a visit to Philadelphia. Oranges from Barcelona were presented—a rarity. One young lady took hers home and carefully pared it into a design for a quilt which is still known as the Lafayette Orange Peel. Courtesy of the Wenham Historical Association and Museum, Wenham, Massachusetts.

seeming to speak of another time and place, and usually a story was involved. I loved the gay colors and the names of the patterns. When my grandmother allowed me to choose one for my very own from her collection, I asked for an old one, and decided on one she had made, a rather faded Turkey red and white. In retrospect, I'm sure it was the name of the pattern that fascinated me. It was called the Darting Minnow, the minnow being a simple small white diamond skipping through the whole design. (Plate 4.) But it was enough to stir the imagination of a child, just as it had evoked imaginative and poetic thinking on the part of the maker, my grandmother.

Quilts were a part of my life even during the years when they were not in fashion. In that section of Tennessee where I grew up in the early part of the twentieth century, quilts still served as a suitable lightweight bedcovering in a moderate climate. We had a goodly supply for "everyday wear," but they were not made at home. They were made by the Witt sisters, two nice maiden ladies who lived in the country and during the winter months "pieced quilt tops on the half." That is, for half the scraps my mother provided they would piece quilt tops for her and the other scraps were theirs to use for themselves. In the fall of the year, Mother took materials left from the family sewing to them; these included bits from our outgrown cotton dresses. Then, in the spring, the finished quilt tops were picked up and taken, along with plain white material for linings, rolls of cotton batting for interlining, and plenty of spools of white cotton thread for quilting, to some elderly lady who still owned a quilting frame and practiced the old art. After the three thicknesses—top, lining, and interlining—were sewed together, the edges were bound and

PLATE 2

Randolph Family Pattern. The original quilt from which this one was copied was brought to Tennessee by the William Randolph family of Virginia when the Randolphs migrated in about 1800. The pattern continues to be passed on through the generations and many descendants have made their copies. The appliquéd top of the quilt pictured here was made in 1930 by the author, a descendant of William Randolph. The quilting (twelve hundred yards of thread) was done by an expert quilter, Mrs. Amanda Taylor of Rockwood, Tennessee. Bacon Collection.

the quilts were ready. I recall that they were quite pretty. The Witt sisters took pride in arranging the scraps in designs, with their delightful names—Dove at the Window, Irish Chain, Hens and Chickens, Dresden Plate—instead of piecing them into crazy or hit-and-miss patterns. I wonder, however, if we appreciated fully the amount of work that had gone into them.

Later in the first quarter of the century, when quilt-making had fallen to an all-time low, something began stirring in our small town of Rockwood which was far reaching in its consequence. This was "Cousin Rebecca's quilt revival"—a wonderful example of what one enthusiastic and imaginative lover of beauty can accomplish.

Mrs. James Fletcher Tarwater (Cousin Rebecca) was a great lady and her home, Elmoak, widely known for its hospitality. Recalling the fine quilts of earlier days which had migrated to Tennessee by way of both Virginia and the Carolinas, she bemoaned the fact that the quality of the few quilts currently being made had deteriorated and she determined to do something about it. So far as I know she was the first person (certainly in our area and in that period) to indulge in the exciting hobby of creating decorative quilts simply because they were beautiful. To see her glowing, colored quilts adorning the four-posters in the spacious, high-ceilinged rooms of Elmoak was a thrilling sight to me.

So, perhaps the answer to the question of how I became interested in quilts reaches far back—as far back as Cousin Rebecca's own family history. In the early eighteen hundreds, William Randolph, our mutual ancestor, came from Virginia to establish his home in the new State of Tennessee. William (a min-

PLATE 3
Red and Green Appliqué Quilt. A sophisticated Philadelphia quilt, c. 1850, distinctive because of a number of features including workmanship, design, and double border. Its very size is impressive (about twelve feet square). It must have required a goodly number of feather mattresses, piled high, to accommodate its generous proportions, and tall steps must have been necessary to mount the bed. Miss Mildred Whittemore of Newton, Massachusetts, inherited the quilt through her grandmother's family and can recall seeing it used on just such a mammoth bed. Turkey red and green was a favorite combination of colors. This rich green with a yellow cast was known as "Victoria Green" in honor of the young Queen Victoria. Courtesy of the Friends of the Jackson Homestead Historical Museum, Newton, Massachusetts.

ister of the Gospel as stated in the family Bible), with his wife, Louisa Bailey Randolph, and young daughter Sarah, made the trip by flatboat down the French Broad River. Along with them there came a quilt of special significance. According to tradition, the design was known as the Randolph family pattern (Plate 2). The quilt was cherished through the years and daughter Sarah, who had become Grandmother Sarah, still delighted in passing on the old traditions, especially to her receptive granddaughter Rebecca. The old quilt, however, suffered the misfortune of being almost destroyed by fire, and the last time Sarah showed it to Rebecca (by then a grown woman with a family of her own), it was in a sad state. Fortunately, enough of the original design had been saved to serve as a challenge to Rebecca. Years later, she decided to make a copy of it, with the result that a Randolph quilt once again became a proud family possession.

Having copied this quilt successfully, Cousin Rebecca's enthusiasm grew. Seeking out other old patterns, she created many beautiful quilts, far exceeding her original aim of making a quilt for each of her children and grandchildren, of which there were a goodly number. She was able to indulge her hobby to the extent that she kept accomplished needlewomen in her home to make elaborate quilt tops. They were quilted by expert quilters, for another important part of Cousin Rebecca's effort was to seek out the few quilters (still remaining in that part of the country) whose work compared favorably with that of previous generations. Thus she kept the art of fine quilting alive and guided many a descendant of Grandmother Sarah in making her own Randolph quilt. And because her generous encouragement also went beyond the bounds of family and kin, there are still to be

PLATE 4
Darting Minnow. Faded red and white quilt, c. 1870. The pattern is full of movement, suggesting the imaginative name—the "minnow" being the simple diamond patch that seems to skip through the whole design. The backing of the quilt is homespun. Made by Sarah Woods Brazeale Ingram of Tennessee, grandmother of the author. Bacon Collection.

found in the Rockwood area unusually lovely quilts of excellent workmanship and design.

It was after I was married and had two children that I felt inspired to attempt making a quilt. My home was in New England but on trips back to Tennessee, I looked at Cousin Rebecca's quilts with fresh admiration and decided to copy her beautiful Rose of Sharon (Plate 48) for my daughter, to be her "Bride's Quilt" after the old custom. Then, for my three-year-old son, I chose the Randolph family pattern for his "Freedom Quilt," carrying out another bit of quilt lore.

I suppose I presented an unusual sight—a young woman working on something as old-fashioned as a quilt. It certainly aroused interest in spite of the fact that quiltmaking was no longer a popular pastime, and people appeared eager to hear about it. I was asked to speak before groups of club and church women. Thus my vocation began, and a most rewarding experience it has been. As time has passed, I have spoken in a number of Middle Atlantic and Southern states, all the New England states, as well as at the American Museum in England.

The aspect of quiltmaking that interested me most was how the quilt seemed to have served not only as a means of providing necessary warmth, but also as an outlet for an inherent longing for beauty and decoration. It was my premise that the making of quilts was the most universal of all the folk arts in early America, appealing to women everywhere and in all walks of life, and experience strengthened that belief. As my concern for the subject deepened, however, I began to wonder. Did this really apply to women in all walks of life, even to those whose lives were exceedingly hard? I became aware that my own involvement and knowledge were confined more or less to quite elaborate quilts, products of pleasant ways of living made by the more privileged women who had leisure hours to spend creating them.

It was in the changing, warring forties that I definitely set out one summer in quest of quilt lore. I turned to the areas of Appalachia. I wanted to talk with women in isolated places who had not been caught up in the accelerated pace of modern times. I wanted to know the part that the making of patchwork quilts had played in their lives and the lives of their foremothers. It was not easy to find them, even though I had a few leads. With the advent of good roads, the isolated places had changed. Furthermore, quilts were out of style and it was hard to find anyone who was the least bit interested. I quite agreed with one native lady who, in answer to my queries, said sympathetically, "Yes, ma'am, they sure are mighty-near plum run out." But with perseverance I was able to locate a few women who could confirm what I had thought.

Among them was "Mother York" of Jamestown, Tennessee, well known as the mother of Sergeant Alvin York, the greatest hero of World War I. She was a woman of poise and strength of character typical of the mountain people. She said she was still making quilts and used to make quilts "on the halves," for scraps were "dear in the mountain parts." She spoke of the warm friendliness that still remained part of "quiltin's and workin's."

Near Horseshoe, North Carolina, I visited with two ladies, "Aunt" Cynthia Creasman and Miss Tiny Edmondson, sympathetic and knowledgeable, both living in secluded homes that had belonged to their forebears. "Aunt Cinnie," as she was called, was a merry soul in her eighties. She had made hundreds of quilts and was still making them "to keep from idling." When people asked why so many, her answer, laughingly, was, "I might marry again and I'd have to have enough for twin beds." When she agreed to sell me a quilt, she said with a twinkle, "If you can count the stitches, I'm a mind to give it to you."

With both Aunt Cinnie and Miss Tiny, it was evident that the making of quilts had been one of the most stimulating and satisfying parts of their lives, reinforcing my theory that the quilt served as an outlet for artistic longings. While Aunt Cinnie said she made up her patterns to fit her scraps, Miss Tiny talked with feeling about how she had cut her paper designs on the floor at night after the day's work was done, "working with them until I got them to fit right." Miss Tiny was a retiring person and when I asked her if I might buy a quilt, her quiet answer was, "No, I don't want to sell." These were her treasures. I doubt if Miss Tiny knew how many quilts were piled in the stacks all around the room in addition to the "chists" full of them. About her prized quilting frame, she remarked, "Me and my mother sawed out the logs for ourselves." Many of the quilts had been made by her mother and Miss Tiny had made her first quilt before she was ten years old. She had never stopped and they were all there—the Temperance Tree, a Save-all, Bird's Nest, and the most difficult of all, she said, the Twisted Chain, a striking example of abstract design.

Sadly enough, warring, changing times are still with us in the seventies. But let us take heart. There surely is a quilt revival today and perhaps with it a revival of concern for tradition and craftsmanship and the special beauty of handmade things.

L.I.B.

I
Genesis:
The Bed and
the Quilt

Indigenous as Vermont maple sugar, picturesque as a split-rail fence in Appalachia, dignified as a New England sea captain's mansion, romantic as the white-pillared plantation houses of the deep South, patchwork is uniquely interwoven with the story of America.

The art of patchwork reached its zenith in the New World in the colorful bed quilt. It combined much of the traditional background of the old, yet reflected a new way of life in a pioneer land. And through the quilt there has been bequeathed to us a very human document, a tracing in fine stitches of the history of these United States.

Within the folds of the quilt are pieced the dreams of the men and women who were wresting a place of their own from the unsubdued wilderness: their hardships and their faith, their playtimes and their workaday lives, their political battles, the deep-moving forces of their religion, the heartbeats of all those who were laying the foundations of a new country.

From the time of the landing of the first settlers and the clearing of the land, the patchwork quilt played an important role in the establishing of homes amid unfamiliar surroundings. A strange blending of the twin goals of practicality and artistry, it served two purposes: the very physical necessity of keeping warm in rudely constructed, mud-daubed houses, and, equally important, the creating of a quilt met a psychological need—serving as an outlet for the pioneer woman's artistic and aesthetic longings.

In its broader scope, however, patchwork is the product of many peoples and civilizations. In order to attempt to trace its history, we must go back much further in time than the settling of America or even our European background. As with many of our domestic arts, its origin is steeped in mystery and can only be partially unraveled. It is as old as Woman, dating to that moment of decision when Eve pieced *two* fig leaves together to conform to the new idea of dress for the human family.

The basic art of pieced work was used by primitive man in contriving his animal-skin garments. After the knowledge of weaving developed, he joined together bits of cloth to cover himself, and, to satisfy his innate desire for decoration, he learned to make dyes and added color to his clothes.

Patchwork consists of two forms. One is the simple piecing together of patches, called "piecing" or "patching." The other is the cutting of one kind of material and laying it upon another in patches, called "applied work" or "appliqué." From these two basic methods of needlework there developed an elaborate and in-

tricate art used with such skill and imagination that it served to decorate man's most precious *objets d'art* throughout the ages.

Perhaps the earliest tangible evidences of patch-work are found in Egypt, which shows that the art flourished there in both forms, pieced and appliqué, as long ago as the time of the Pharaohs. The Museum of Cairo claims to have the oldest example of patch-work still in existence. Fashioned from a gazelle hide and composed of beautifully colored pieces, it served as the canopy for an Egyptian queen about 960 B.C.[1]

The early Egyptians were proud of their inventive faculties and renowned for their knowledge of dyes and mordants. Their skill in harmonizing and pre-serving colors is seen in mummy cases, wrappings, and paintings preserved within their tombs. The Egyptians excelled in the manufacture of fine fabrics —linen, cotton, and wool—creating beautiful and striking works of art through the use of such ma-terials. They used applied work and "broideries of gold" to fashion paneled screens that vividly portrayed the things they loved and the gods they worshiped. Asps were entwined on the borders to signify royalty. From luxurious hangings, depicting life-size figures, lions' heads, sacred serpents, gazelles, and from car-touches with inscriptions, we catch glimpses of the way of life in the days of the Ramses, Ptolemys, and Cleopatra.

Patchwork is popular in modern Egypt. Tourists can find simple patchwork pieces that use ancient designs and sacred emblems of the past, such as the lotus flower, the winged beetle, scarabs, and discs that signify sun worship. From these copies one can recapture some of the splendor of ancient Egypt

Genesis: The Bed and the Quilt

that reached out and affected the civilizations of the world.

The children of the Israelites during their long years of captivity in Egypt were intimately exposed to the grandeurs with which their masters surrounded themselves. As laborers they learned the intricacies of the decorative arts and the Egyptian secrets of making dyes and textiles. At the time of their exodus to freedom they took with them a legacy of great beauty along with the knowledge to perpetuate that beauty.

The Book of Ezekiel in the Bible contains a direct reference to this influence. The prophet sings in extravagant praise of the glories of Tyre:

> O Tyrus, . . . Thy borders are in the midst of the seas, thy builders have perfected thy beauty. . . . Fine linen with broidered work from Egypt was that which thou spreadest forth to be thy sail; blue and purple from the isles of Elishah was that which covered thee.[2]

It is therefore not surprising that Israel's daughters should have been proficient in the art of the needle as practiced in Egypt. When Herod the Great rebuilt the Temple of Jerusalem "careful not to omit in the decoration of the sanctuary the marvels of textile art,"[3] in all likelihood it was the descendants of Egypt's captives who were responsible for creating the dramatic effects of the great hangings that embellished it, employing the same kinds of fabrics as well as the symbolic colors of Egyptian adornment: "Scarlet signified fire; linen, the earth; azure, the air; and purple, the sea."[4]

During the centuries that followed the flight from Egypt, patchwork and "broidery" combined with the

PLATE 5
Sampler or Legacy Quilt. This multi-colored New England sampler quilt, designed for use on a four-poster, is made up of a collection of the designs popular in the early part of the nineteenth century. This type of quilt was sometimes also called a Legacy quilt. In every village there were quiltmakers galore, but always there was one a little more outstanding than any other. She became an authority and had her own collection of templates for drawing complicated designs. In fact, she was referred to as the "master quilter." Often, as time was running out, she would make what might be her last quilt, featuring patterns that she considered worthy of being passed on. This was her legacy. Offen Collection.

fine art of quilting spread throughout the Eastern world, resulting in a rich mingling of cultures. The needlewomen of Syria received fresh inspiration for their own native ability and produced designs in applied work identical to those transplanted by the Hebrews. Arabian women, renowned for their quilting, influenced the arts of Persia, where there are preserved some of the finest examples of quilting of the Middle Ages. Developed in typical oriental manner, quilting was combined with all types of needlework to enhance and embellish their prayer rugs, carpets, and hangings of silk, linen, and satin.

By the time the Crusaders had arrived in the Near East, the art of needlework had reached an incredible state of perfection. As the Crusaders, representatives of the most influential and intelligent men of the Western world, pressed their way into Eastern countries, they discovered refinements of living often surpassing their own. Treasures exquisite beyond description were eagerly carried home to their womenfolk. An active commerce between East and West was established, and Eastern merchants brought their priceless wares into Spain, France, Italy, Germany, and England.

The decorative arts entered into an exciting period of development in Western Europe that lasted throughout the Middle Ages. Spinning, weaving, and dyeing received fresh impetus. The arts of patchwork, quilting, and embroidery flourished. Gorgeous materials were used—satins, silks, brocades, even leather and lace—often accented by precious jewels. Women in all walks of life participated. Queens and noble ladies within their walled castles as well as women in peasant cottages worked to bring color and art into their lives.

Beautiful and spectacular decorations were made for the churches and cathedrals. Because of the emphasis on the church in the Middle Ages, no amount of time was considered too much to lavish upon fashioning hangings, altar cloths, religious banners, and other accessories. So much work went into the making of ecclesiastical vestments that at least one ruling bishop upbraided his priests for "wearing their religion on their backs rather than in their hearts."[5]

Credit for the introduction of patchwork hangings into the great churches of Italy has sometimes been given to the Florentine painter Alessandro Botticelli (1444–1510). Inspired by the exquisite work of the Armenians, called "thought-work" because everything that went into it was meaningful, Botticelli copied their designs on elaborate hangings for church decorations. Later these patchwork hangings were replaced by his mural paintings and tapestries renowned for their great beauty.

Special love went into the making of garments for the Crusaders as they set about their holy missions. They wore much quilted clothing under their chain mail, and their cloaks and banners were elaborately appliquéd. Their standards, carrying the armorial bearings of the proudest families of Western Europe, often displayed the symbol of the cross wrought in the finest needlework.

These were long and anxious periods of time with their men away in foreign lands fighting Holy Wars, and the women needed to keep their minds occupied

as well as their fingers. While they lavished their talents on the churches and the cathedrals, they also found pleasure and comfort in creating furnishings for their own homes—handsome wall hangings, draperies, and bed dressings. And, since the twin arts of patchwork and quilting always lend themselves especially to the making of fine bedcovering, so the women of the Middle Ages developed the art of quilt-making to an almost unbelievable degree of elaboration and beauty. Small wonder, since the bed was recognized as the most important piece of furniture in the medieval home.

THE BED AND THE QUILT

From the time when the simple bed, set in the middle of the tent, dominated the life of the nomadic tribes, to the Middle Ages when the great four-posters of Tudor days commanded the place of honor in the center of the great halls, the bed has been the most important and significant of man's household furnishings.

> It was the resting place for tired humanity and around it centers the romance of domestic life. . . . It is in the evolution of the bedstead that the connoisseur tries to picture the domestic home life of the ages which have gone. He pieces the story little by little from the scanty evidence left.[6]

Guy de Maupassant goes much further in his definition of the bed. "The bed is our whole life. It is there that we are born, it is there that we love, it is there that we die."

Interwoven with the history of the bed is that of the bed quilt. In fact, the quilt has sometimes served as man's bed as well as equipment for it. Webster's dictionary defines it as a "rectangular piece of material laid out for comfort in lying down." In early days a pad could be a quilt stuffed with rags, tow or hair scraped from hides of animals, matted down to form a crude felt. Nor is recycling new; in the life of early New England it was known as "making things do."

There are Gloucester fishermen today who remember the layered quilts or pads made for them by their womenfolk to take to sea with them. Composed of layers of whatever materials had been obtainable, one side was covered with soft and woolly pieces patched together to serve as protective covering against the cold. The reverse side was composed of patches of hard, closely woven cloth. These served as beds (pads or pallets) and in summer were more cooling than the hot boards of the deck.

In attempting to trace the origins of both bed and quilt, we must delve far back into the history of mankind before the written word. We know that man's first bed was wherever he chose to lie, its literal meaning "a dug-out place," filled with leaves, grass or moss to ease his bones, the hides of animals to give him warmth. After man had succeeded in housing himself, we learn that his beds were "sacks filled with straw or chaff placed upon the floor or upon an oaken chest."[7]

William Harrison, the English historian of the sixteenth century, wrote in reference to beds in old England:

Our fathers have lien full oft upon straw pallets or rough mats covered only with a sheet and under the

coverlet made of dogswain with a good round log under their heads instead of a bolster or pillow. As for their servants, if they had one sheet above them it was well, for seldome they had anie under, to keep them from the pricking straw that ran oft through the canvas of the pallet and raised their hardened hides.[8]

This unhappy state applied, no doubt, to many unfortunates of the time who considered themselves lucky to have a stuffed sack of any kind. Those who could afford greater comfort softened their resting places with feathers, animal skins, and furs. Perhaps here was where the feminine influence began asserting itself, for after all, beds usually constitute a partnership.

As time went on and man's artistic sense developed along with a desire for comfort, the bed was elevated above the floor and a more protective arrangement evolved. Bed recesses, upon which a "culcita" or quilt could be laid, were built into the wall and were often curtained for privacy and greater warmth. Bed niches are to be found in some of the houses unearthed at Pompeii.

Such "resting places for tired humanity" are a far cry from the grandeur of beds and their accompanying accessories that have been prepared for the high and the mighty in all the great civilizations of the world. We stand in awe of the lavishness of the elaborately decorated beds of the Egyptians, the metal and ivory inlaid beds of the Assyrians, the gold and silver inlaid designs that embellished the beds of the Medes and the Persians, the bronze bedsteads of the Roman rulers, the solid silver beds of the Indian princes. Certain characteristics marked nearly all such resting places. They were dressed with rich

PLATE 6
Overall Star Pattern. Star names for quilts easily led the list in popularity. This magnificent example from Vermont of an all-encompassing pattern is referred to as The Star of Bethlehem, Star of the East, and, in Texas, The Lone Star. It is also called The Rising Sun, which is a picturesque title for it and was the name given it in 1839 by the maker, Mary Jane Bartlett.
Offen Collection.

hangings, and were so high that they had to be ascended by steps.

In different countries beds were expressive of the times and the locale, from the richly gilded Italian beds of the Renaissance to the extravagant ceremonial beds of the French court; the elaborately carved beds of the Dutch and Germans to the sumptuous beds of Spain and Portugal.

One writer, in describing an impressive Spanish bed, attempts to describe the proper way of approaching such a formidable piece of furniture:

> Hangings of satin, brocade, and rich skins were used in conjunction with gold and silver embroidery, whilst a triptych or driptych containing the sacred images was placed at the head end; balustrades of wood, heavily silvered, were around it and steps of silver provided that it might be entered without loss of dignity.[9]

In the days when family life centered in the main part of the house or the great hall, where there were warmth and companionship, separate bedchambers were not provided. The beds of the well-to-do in Western countries played an important role by day as well as by night. Placed in the great hall in the central living quarters of the house, the bed served as a mammoth couch, the focal point in a way of life.

Bedsteads continued to increase in importance, reflecting prevailing style trends not only in household furnishings but also in changing customs. The comparatively simple type of bed composed of canopy and tester progressed during the Middle Ages and the Tudor Oak days to become impressive four-posters.

Expenditures on state beds in palaces was exceed-

PLATE 7
Birds in Flight. Another name for this pattern that also suggests dramatic movement is Wild Geese Flying. This quilt was made in 1825 and is in perfect condition. Only a portion of it is shown. The hundreds of soaring triangles, cut from fascinating cloth, give an idea of the amazing richness of the early nineteenth-century calicoes from which quiltmakers could choose. Calico was supreme in patchwork, its soft texture and lovely colorings peculiarly adapted to the art. There were background colors swirled and overlaid with unusual combinations of fruit and flowers, intricate Persian effects in colorings little known or used today—plum, snuff, maroon, puce, China-blue, and black-green. The lining of this quilt is a delightful warm gray with prints of small feathers and flowers in rusty orange and brown. The maker was probably Mrs. William H. Simon and the quilt was presented to the Jackson Homestead by C. M. Simon. Courtesy of the Friends of the Jackson Homestead Historical Museum, Newton, Massachusetts.

Genesis: The Bed and the Quilt

ingly great. Choicest treasures in needlework were to be found in ladies' bedchambers. In the reign of Elizabeth I, counterpanes, embroidered and hand-painted in India and Persia, were used. Shakespeare in *Cymbeline* wrote of "the adornment of Imogen's bed, her bedchamber hung with tapestry of silk and silver."[10] Charles II of England paid eight thousand pounds to furnish bed hangings and bedroom furniture for his queen at Hampton Court, while in France the cost for Marie Antoinette's bed, embroidered with pearls and other precious adornments, was 131,820 livres.[11]

Lavishness bestowed upon the bed was not confined to the wealthy, however. Harrison, the historian, writing of Elizabethan days, says:

> The use of costly furniture has descended even into the inferior artificers, and many farmers who have learned to garnish their joyned beds with tapestrie and silk hangings, whereas our fathers, yea and we ourselves, have lain full oft upon straw pallets . . . and a good round log for a pillow.[12]

Samuel Pepys, the English diarist, whose *Diary* gives witness to his complete harmony with the animalism and vulgarity of the Restoration, attests to the work and devotion bestowed by his wife Elizabeth Marchant upon their bed furnishings. He records: "Home to my poor wife, who works all day like a horse, at the making of her hangings for our chamber and bed."[13] In spite of another entry in the *Diary* that he had "kicked the cook and blacked my wife's eye," it is evident from his frequent entries "and so to bed" that his resting place was one of comfort and satisfaction in his home.

From the earliest stages in the evolution of the bed,

curtains were considered necessary, and "under the curtains" was a common expression for "in bed." It was impossible for a husband to escape a wifely "curtain lecture"—and there was something to be said in its favor: At least the lady waits until she can give her lecture privately. The "curtain lecture" was still routine in Charles Dickens' day. Dickens gave some inspiration on the subject to his close friend Douglas Jerrold, which resulted in Jerrold's version, *Mrs. Caudle's Curtain Lectures.*

In the castles of the mighty, affairs of state were carried on from beds. Ceremonial beds placed in the *chambre de parade* were considered more appropriate from which to receive important ambassadors and great lords, a greater compliment to those being received. Petitions were heard from the "beds of justice." The *lit de justice* has been defined as the "custom of a king, dictator, high priest or other persons of great authority who issued edicts and judgments to a formal assembly of his subordinates from his bed," not necessarily the one in which he usually slept but a reclining "seat of justice," elaborate in design and decoration. Louis XI has been credited for its introduction into the Western world, and a *grand lit* was provided for him wherever he stayed. Using it whenever he appeared in Parliament, it presented an impressive picture—the King of France reclining on a Bed of Justice, raised on a dais which was approached by seven steps carpeted in blue velvet embroidered in golden fleurs de lis. The arrangement around the bed denoted royal power and rank—the princes standing, the great officials seated, and the lesser officials kneeling.

Just when the custom of dispensing justice from

Genesis: The Bed and the Quilt

the bed began is not definitely known. It has been claimed, however, that the issuing of authority from the bed goes back into history much further than medieval times and Louis XI.

From fragments of the Greek historian Phylarchus in the third century B.C., we read how Alexander the Great "transacted business reclining on a golden bed in the middle of a gigantic tent, his troops and attendants, two thousand or more, drawn up in order around him."[14] Also there is traditional evidence that not only emperors and high officials of the Roman empire but tribal leaders of the Neolithic Age gave audience in the same reclining position.[15]

The use of the *lit de justice* was restricted at first to royal personages, but the idea was so attractive with its combination of ease and authority that in time it became widespread and much less formal. The space between the bed and the wall called the "ruelle" proved to be such a delightful place in which to receive intimates that a morning reception held in their bedrooms by fashionable French ladies during the seventeenth and eighteenth centuries came to be called a "ruelle."

Curious customs arose as part of the "etiquette of the bed." It was the fashion for great ladies, upon occasions thought deserving of special congratulations or condolences, to receive their friends from their beds. In Versailles, this was quite proper even directly after a marriage.

The beds of kings and queens were saluted and paid homage as if they were altars rivaling the throne. None approached them, even when there was no railing to prevent it. However, reasons other than ceremonial

PLATE 8
Stars Within Stars. A quilt containing twenty-five stars surrounded by star designs, of "Turkey red" and white. The date is probably mid-nineteenth century, and the quilt is from the Woodward Homestead, built in 1689, the second oldest house in the town of Newton, Massachusetts. Bacon Collection.

Genesis: The Bed and the Quilt

have been given for the use of railings. Old accounts of life in several fifteenth-century castles mention railings to keep dogs from the beds.

In times conducive to great intimacy, there was intrigue and freedom in the matter of morals. An atmosphere of illusion and allurement was cultivated. It became the style to appear *en deshabille*. Roger de Felice in his writing discloses a rather interesting and amusing aspect of modesty. In entertaining from the bed, whatever else might have been exposed, the ladies kept their feet covered. To quote M. de Felice, "At a period of so much license the ladies, far from showing their bare feet, were expected to conceal them with a coverlet of embroidered silk as a concession to decency."[16] Is it any wonder that the coverlet or quilt should have assumed such importance, fitting into such a role in the luxurious bedchamber of a lady of style?

As women aspired to beautify their resting places, the making of quilts and coverlets became the most absorbing activity whether in castle or cottage.

II
Gleanings
from Patchwork
History

As we continue our attempt to trace the history of the bed quilt, we gather our scanty bits of information wherever we can find them, piecing them into a patchwork story, just as the quiltmakers of old gathered their precious scraps of cloth and fashioned them into a patchwork coverlet.

Fortunately, some rare examples of quiltmaking of historical significance, expressive of many ages and cultures, have survived. These serve as clues, indicating the character and personality of those who made them, as well as the background of their regions.

It is only natural that those quilts which have survived the ravages of time should be the handsome, the unusual, or the beautiful, for the obvious reason that they have been considered worthy of preserving and have been given special care through the years. Such are the fourteenth-century examples of Sicilian cord quilting, depicting elaborate scenes from the legend of Tristan, done on linen using brown thread. (The development of trapunto and the use of it in the making of quilts has been attributed to the artistry of early Italian needleworkers.)

Among the fine coverlets surviving the Middle Ages are silk and damask quilts so popular in France and Italy; quilts suitable for the colder climates of Germany and Holland, made of heavy brocades and velvets; notable quilts of museum quality which give evidence of Portuguese, Sicilian, and Turkish origins; the costly counterpanes of royal purple embroidered in gold and designed for heavy Roman beds.

Old records of the French Revolution reveal a description of a quilt made for the lighthearted young French queen, Marie Antoinette. As a part of her bridal finery, the quilt was eight years in the making. Elaborately appliquéd with flowers, cupids, and other love motifs, it was quilted by the ladies of the court of her mother, Maria Theresa, in Austria. Later, when France was in a state of bankruptcy and the unfortunate queen was beset by angry accusers, the French Revolutionary Tribunal cited the quilt as just one more example of her excessive extravagances.[1]

Mary Stuart, Queen of Scots, and her devotion to needlework is a well-known story. She became proficient in the arts of lacemaking, embroidery, and appliqué as a young girl in France, and learned the art of quilting while living at the court of Catherine de' Medici. At the time of her imprisonment, Mary Stuart took with her into prison two of the embroiderers maintained in her service. During the long years that followed, plying her needle gave her comfort and diversion. Her slender fingers fashioned exquisite quilts, some of which can be viewed at

PLATE 9

Opposite: *Early Ohio Quilt. The unusual arrangement of triangles results in an intricate and original design, with staid browns and blacks set off by fresh blues and reds. This is an example of a "quilt-painting" of the sort that so much interests collectors today. Made in the first half of the nineteenth century by Susan Gregg Cochran, of Quaker parentage, in Quaker City, Ohio.* Bacon Collection.

PLATE 10

Overleaf: *Log Cabin. A woolen tied quilt done in the Log Cabin pattern long popular with quiltmakers. The central block in each pieced design denotes the chimney of the log cabin. This excellent example was made by Mrs. Samuel Gardner of Maine in the early 1800's.* Courtesy of her granddaughter, Katherine Reynolds Day.

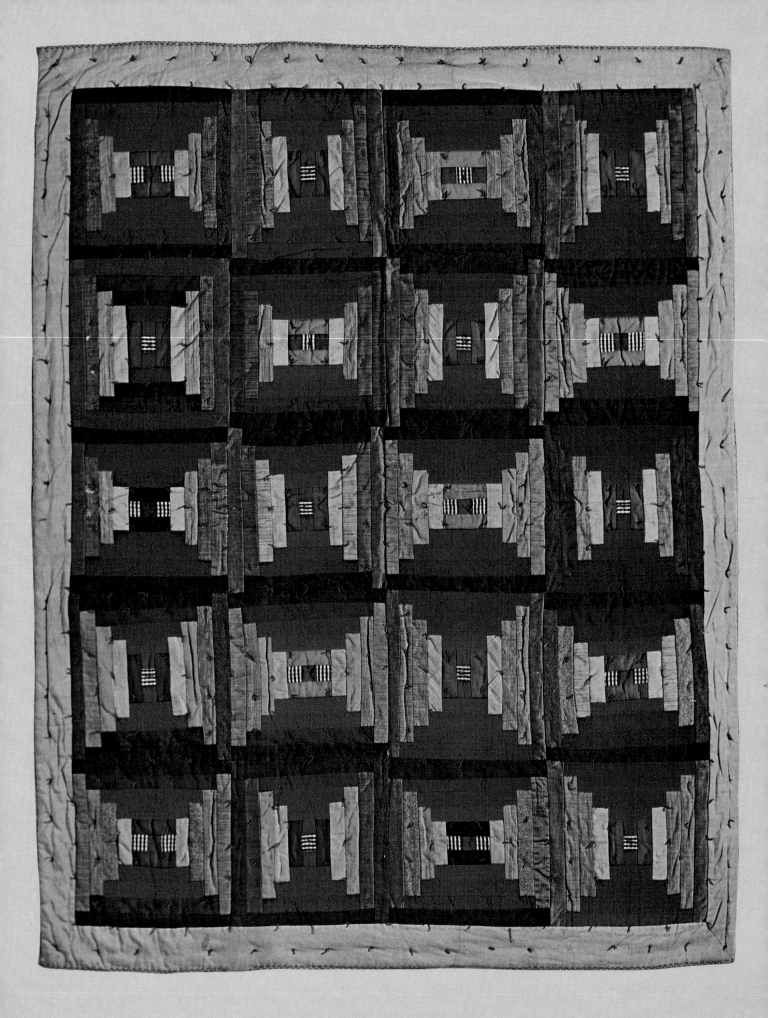

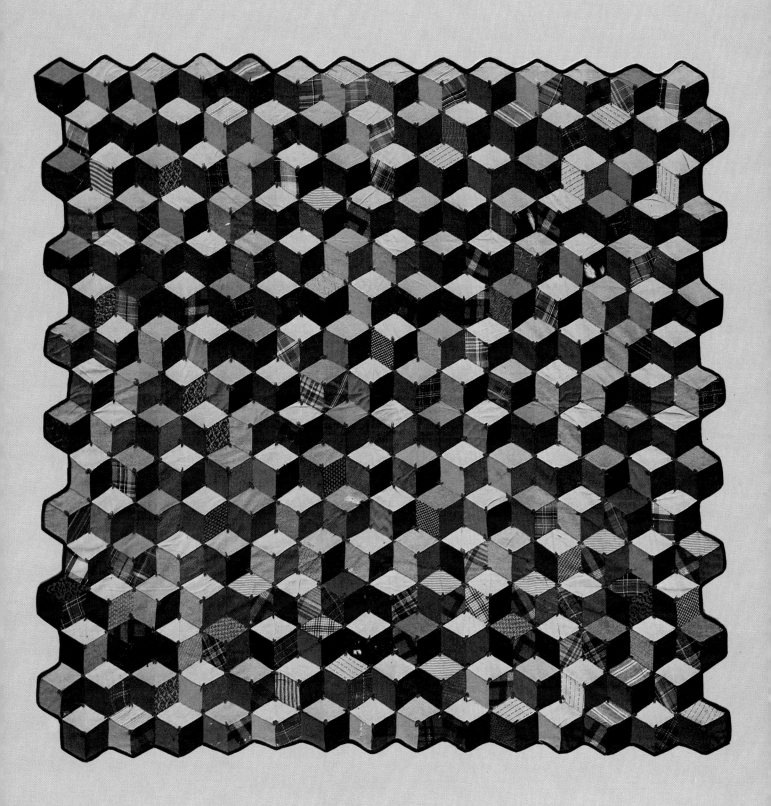

Hardwick Hall in England. On being asked how the Queen passed her time while confined, an attendant wrote:

> that all day she wrought with her nydil and that the diversity of the colours made the work seem less tedious and that she contynued so long at it that veray payn made hir to give over.[2]

Catherine of Aragon, the Spanish wife of Henry VIII, also an indefatigable needlewoman, is given credit for introducing the popular "black work" into England. This consisted of a black silk outline stitch admirably suited to giving greater durability to quilts. It was called Spanish work after the Queen, but in all probability its origin is much more remote, having found its way from Persia and China to the Western world by way of the Moors and the Crusaders.[3]

Perhaps in no part of Western Europe did the twin arts of patchwork and quilting, along with other forms of needlecraft, flourish so productively as in Jacobean England. John Taylor, an English pamphleteer, commonly called the "Water Poet," published in 1640 a poem called "The Prayse of the Needle," so popular that it ran through twelve editions:

> To all dispersed sorts of Arts and Trades
> I write the needles prayse (that never fades)
> So long as children shall be begot and borne,
> So long as Hemp or Flax shall be made and worne,
> So long as silk-worms, with exhausted spoile,
> Of their own entrailes for man's gain shall toyle;
> Yes, till the world be quite dissolved and past,
> So long, at least, the Needles use shall last.

"Working fine arts with a needle" came to be a necessary part of a girl's education, often to the exclusion of reading and writing. Lady Montagu, wife of

the Duke of Montagu, Master of the Great Wardrobe to William III, wrote, "It is as scandalous for a woman not to know how to use a needle as it is for a man not to know how to use a sword."[4] She stressed especially the importance of young women spending time working on their bed hangings and coverlets.

Women lavished their talents on everything from waistcoats for their men to the fabulous gowns for the nobility—so appliquéd, quilted, and heavily covered with gold and silver that they could almost stand alone. Queen Elizabeth's wardrobe at the time of her death contained more than a thousand dresses, each a real production. Besides the gold and silver quilting and embroidery, they were hung with bullion, pearls, and jewels. Little wonder that train bearers were such an important part of her court. Even Elizabeth, strong character that she was, might stagger under such a load.[5]

Old chronicles give us an insight into what was cherished by telling us that in 1540 Catherine Howard, when she married Henry VIII, was presented with twenty-three closely quilted quilts from the royal wardrobe.[6]

Elizabethan inventories often mentioned quilts. Among the possessions of Robert Dudley, Earl of Leicester, at Kenilworth in 1584, were several elaborate quilts, one described as "a faire quilte of crymson satin . . . all lozenged over with silver twiste . . . fringed aboute with a small fringe of crymson silke, lined through with white fustian."[7]

Quilts were imported into England as early as 1631 from the East Indies and China.[8] Made of taffeta embroidered in gold or Pitania embroidered in silk ". . . . of deep red grounds and other sadder colours. . . ."

They sold for £ 5 5s to £ 6 the pair. Rich quilted material also was sold by the yard or length.

A quilt which is said to have been made by Queen Anne is preserved at Madresfield Court.[9] Perhaps she and her intimate friend, first lady of the bedchamber, Sarah Churchill, happily plied their needles together. This would have been during the time when their relationship was harmonious. Their deep intimacy had foundered long before 1720, partly because of Sarah's impetuosity and high temper. But Sarah, Duchess of Marlborough, was no doubt just as imperious as ever when, in 1720, she gave an order for "a vast number of feather beds to be made, some filled with swansdown, and also a vast number of quilts"[10] for her house.

In the Middle Ages, patchwork was not enjoyed by the wealthy alone. Applied work was a cheaper substitute for embroidery and for tapestry. It has been referred to as "the peasant art." The Victoria and Albert Museum's *Notes on Quilting* also says, "The use of the word *quilt* can be traced back as far as the thirteenth century at least, and so the making of quilts is undoubtedly an old traditional craft of the British Isles."[11]

There was a saying in Devon that if a girl had not made a quilt before she was twenty-one, no man would want to marry her, and that dire warning in rhyme is still quoted:

> At your quilting, maids, don't dally,
> Quilt quick if you would marry.
> A maid who is quiltless at twenty-one
> Never shall greet her bridal sun!

Today in many of the great country houses that bear testimony to the centuries of England's prosperity and gracious living, treasured quilts are shown with the same pride with which the ancestral silver and family portraits are shown. Spectacular dressings for the bed are an intimate and prominent part of the rich furnishings. Interesting examples of coverlets are guarded with zealous care in the museums.

At ancient Kirkstall Abbey, a Cistercian House, founded in 1172 by Henry deLacey in the valley of Aire, fine examples of early English needlework are preserved under glass. Among these examples is a notable quilt done in the mosaic pattern of pieced minute patches, the ancestor of our American pattern, Grandmother's Flower Garden. The pattern has been universally used wherever quiltmakers are to be found.

At Althorp Park, the home of many generations of Spencers since the seventeenth century, Lord and Lady Spencer point out the unique dairy house, built by the second Lord Spencer, on the grounds of the six-hundred-acre park, completely tiled with tiles made at the original Josiah Wedgwood potteries. With equal enthusiasm they show one of the guest bedrooms decorated in antique patchwork done in silk in the old familiar Block design. The decor includes curtains for the mammoth Tudor four-poster and a matching quilt, as well as window draperies and upholstered chair seats in the same design of patchwork. This widely known pattern has come down to us in America as Baby's Blocks, Building Blocks, Steps to the Altar. It is also sometimes known as Cube Work and is one of those patterns that gives an optical illusion. As one studies it, it can assume the form of stars, blocks, compasses, or cubes. (Plates 11 and 36).

In the picturesque city of Bath, once the great Roman city of Aquae Sulis, is Claverton Manor, a

handsome country house built in 1820, where Sir Winston Churchill as a young man made his first political speech in 1897. This is now the home of the American Museum in Britain. Opened in 1961, the museum was created to increase Anglo-American understanding and is the one museum in Europe containing only American treasures. Interiors from American houses form the effective background depicting life in the New World from the late seventeenth to the middle of the nineteenth century. Outstanding among the exhibits is a superb collection of quilts. There tourists from all over the world may view fine examples of our own patchwork Americana returned to the Mother Country through the generosity of the American Friends of the Museum.

I had the privilege of speaking on the subject of "Patchwork Americana" at this beautiful museum in the summer of 1969. Quilts belonging to the museum, together with a few of my own which I had carried across the ocean for the occasion, were harmoniously displayed as a background for the eventide talk. My George Washington's Plumes (Plate 31) seemed especially at home in English surroundings. Not only is the charming formal flower garden within the spacious grounds a replica of Martha Washington's own garden at Mount Vernon, but there was another reason: The pattern itself was no doubt English-inspired. Tradition has it that the gay feathers and the sweeping plumes incorporated in the making of quilts originated in Northumberland and were reminiscent of colorful costumes of the Court and had a definite connection with royalty. Even though we had broken away from England through a bloody revolution, we Americans were still close to the Mother Country in many of our ideas.

III
European Origins of the Quilt

With such a rich heritage of needlecraft from their forebears, combined with the need to build up an adequate supply of bedcovers, it is not surprising that the women who crossed the seas to America should have immediately emphasized the *contriving* of quilts.

It was also natural that the colonists living under British rule should have looked to the Mother Country for inspiration in many things: the building of their houses, the designing of their furniture and, of course, the making of their quilts.

Of quilts in England, Elizabeth Glaister has written:

> Perhaps no form of secular needlework gave our ancestors so much pleasure in the making or when made, as the quilt or bed coverlet.

It must not be implied, however, that the English alone introduced the quilt to the new land. Just as America is a composite of people from many nations, the quilt as it developed amid fresh surroundings became a blending of a great medley of peoples. It would indeed be an "error to suggest that a nation made up of people from so many homelands of Europe as is America has not been influenced to some extent by all of them."[1]

However, the Spaniards, who were among the first to come, left little if any evidence of the art of patchwork so popular in the Spain of King Ferdinand and Queen Isabella. They were usually adventurers seeking gold and land with no intent of founding homes. Also, they were attracted to the southern part of the New World where the need to acquire a supply of warm bedcoverings was not one of their problems.

The early French settlers who came by way of Canada secured protection against the biting northern winters under covers made of fur, easily obtainable in the great woods surrounding them. Then, too, they seldom brought their families with them, so that the exquisite, delicate needlework of France played no important part in the domestic pursuits of Early America.

Marie D. Webster, in her comprehensive book *Quilts: Their Story and How to Make Them,* makes the statement, "Extensive investigation indicates that the introduction of patchwork and quilting into America was due to the English and Dutch colonists, whose primary object was to found homes."[2] This may be true to a great extent, and in all likelihood it was the memory of quilts left in the comfortable homelands of England and Holland that exerted a very great influence upon the development of the quilt in America. We can imagine that many a lonely

European Origins of the Quilt

woman, recalling the days of Merry England or the coziness and safety of a neat Dutch house, attempted to transplant some of the remembered beauty into the piecing of a Hands Across the Sea coverlet or a Wind-blown Tulip quilt. Many examples of interesting quilts that attest to both the Dutch and English influences are found up and down the eastern seaboard.

Perhaps no one group succeeded in stamping a more indelible mark of superiority in many forms of needlework than did the hardy peoples of German and Dutch stock, and their crafts have remained expressive of their national character. Many distinctive quilts of Dutch origin, bold in design and in combination of colors, reveal the early life of Long Island, Staten Island, and the days of old New York.

The handicrafts of the Pennsylvania Dutch are renowned. Their art of quiltmaking not only has survived, but it continues to flourish, keeping alive the traditional and meaningful patterns: the pineapple for hospitality and the pomegranate for fruitfulness. Just as the tulip had been the symbol of love in Persia, the various tulip patterns so reminiscent of their native land were especially beloved. It was to Holland that the tulip bulb had been imported from Persia, and was said at the time to be worth the price of a coach-and-four. The cultivation of the bulb to a state of perfection made of it a way of life for the Dutch people and a favorite motif in their art. The Mennonites brought it to Pennsylvania, and it became a favorite in the New World gardens and in the world of quiltmaking. The star patterns are still popular, often similar in design to the old hex signs.[3]

PLATE 13
Maltese Cross. This quilt, done in subtle shadings of rose, is pieced of very fine patches. When the outerfaces of the "croix formée" are indented with a V, it is called Cross of Eight Points. I like to think of the design as stemming from the Island of Malta, which was an important crossroads of many civilizations from the dawn of maritime trade. We know that the art of quilting was highly developed in the Mediterranean areas as early as the fourteenth century. Notable examples are to be found in Sicily. Laurenzi Collection.

Nowhere in the new land did the making of quilts take on greater significance than among the English, Irish, and Scottish highlanders who pressed their way ever farther into the mountainous regions of Appalachia to establish their homes. Along with their ballads, their folklore, their fierce pride, and Elizabethan ways, they had brought from their old countries a knowledge of making "bed kivvers." And to the present day, perhaps there is no section in the United States richer in folklore and crafts than the Appalachian Mountains.

But, whatever the European influences and however strong they may have been, we know that the pioneer women of America did not have the means to copy their European forebears for long, even had they desired to.

Few settlers could have indulged in the luxury of imported manufactured cloth such as that described by Benjamin Franklin in a letter to his wife, written from London in 1758:

> I am sending 56 yards of cotton curiously printed from copper plate, for the beds and hangings of our great room.

Many European quilts were made of large layers of materials to match their bed-curtains, with the quilting the principal decorative feature. In all probability this would have been the manner in which the Franklin bed would have been treated.

Such plentitude of cloth, however, was not available in the new land even if it could have been afforded. But this fact did not prevent the pioneer woman from using any material that could be utilized to create bedcovering for her household, even though it meant piecing together whatever scraps were at hand by the light of candles. And, for those women in the lower economic bracket who might not have candles, the use of pine knots was resorted to.

Perhaps nothing can make us realize more vividly the plight of our early settlers and the value of their home-grown cloth and the ingenuity upon which they were forced to draw than the homely words of the "Forefather's Song," composed probably about 1630 and attributed to a member of the Plymouth Colony.

> And now our garments begin to grow thin
> And wool is much wanted to card and to spin
> If we can get a garment to cover without
> Our other in-garments are clout upon clout.[4]
> Our clothes we brought with us are apt to be torn,
> They need to be clouted soon after they're worn,
> But clouting our garments they hinder us nothing—
> Clouts double are warmer than single whole clothing.[5]

The ability to piece "clout upon clout" was important indeed for our foremothers—a very necessary form of patchwork! And the patchwork quilt, contrived of "clouts," tiny "bits and pieces," "snippets and swatches"—even the unworn parts of worn-out garments, was carefully nurtured. An American product, born of necessity![6]

There could be no piecing, however, before there were patches to piece. There must first be the cloth. The task of making a patchwork quilt for many a pioneer woman meant, first of all, growing the flax or cotton, or even raising sheep to provide the raw materials for working. After that came the carding, spinning, and weaving.

To satisfy her longing for color, a woman had to

be proficient in the art of dyeing. (The phrase *dyed-in-the-wool* means dyed before spinning.) This art involved not only concocting the colors but acquiring a more-or-less scientific knowledge of mordants for fixing (or setting) the colors.

The Latin root of mordant, *mordere*, means "to bite" and, according to Mary Frances Davidson in her fascinating booklet, *The Dye-Pot,* "The old dyers once thinking that the dye bit into the fibers, great stress was placed upon proper mordanting." It was imperative to know the proper proportions of salt, vinegar, soda, and other mordants to use in preparing the dye bath. It is said that urine was one of the most effective mordants. The whole process was slow and tedious. In preparing wool for dyeing, "The mordanting may go on over a period of a week, boiling the wool each day in the mordant bath for one-half hour and hanging the wool in a dark, damp place between times."[8] One learned the hard way that too much alum would make wool harsh and sticky, that tin improperly used as a mordant could result in wool brittle enough to break. It was good to know that cream of tartar helped to produce clear, bright colors.

Following the mordanting all materials must be thoroughly washed to avoid "crocking" (rubbing off). Nature's own rainwater was best for the dye-mixing, and certainly Nature was the dyer's truest guide. To quote Frances Van Arsdale Skinner, authority on herbs and flowers, "Much of a woman's knowledge was and still is instinctive—stemming from a common knowledge since the Garden of Eden, when it became Eve's lot to clothe her children."[9]

Naturally, the pioneer woman knew she must "set

the blue pot" in August when indigo was blooming. She learned, probably through trial and error, that "hick'ry bark'll make the lastingest yeller," that madder root was an unfailing source, not only for pink but for that most popular of all quilt colors, Turkey red. Pokeberries produced lovely lavenders; walnut juice and butternut hulls were for making fast blacks and browns; cedar root made a royal purple, and cockleburr, "the prettiest of weeds," produced a rich deep gold. Joe-Pye weed, named for a New England Indian doctor, flaunted in its mauve flower-heads a dye which, when combined with chrome as a mordant, resulted in a deep yellow. The tea shrub served double purposes during the Revolutionary period—as a substitute for tea and a source for a brown or cinnamon-colored dye. Gray was obtained from sumac with copperas, and descendants of the Scottish highlanders might remember that dandelion roots had been used to obtain a magenta for their tartans in the old days.

The lady of the house did not have to move far to gather supplies for her dye pot. They were practically at her doorstep—lily-of-the-valley or Queen Anne's lace for a delicate yellow, marigolds for a deep orange, hollyhocks for a good red, and, of course, there would be larkspur for blue as well as indigo. In her kitchen there were onion skins holding a potential for a deep rust color, and even spinach made a greenish yellow.

But it was not as easy as just reaching out for the source. The following table is proof that it required large quantities to dye even one pound of wool:

Barks—1 peck finely chopped
Leaves—¾ peck, dried

Hulls—1 peck

Flowers—1½ quarts dried flower heads[10]

Mistletoe contained a high green dye content, but it grew tall and was often inaccessible. The making of green remained the most baffling of all colors, being a combination of the two basic colors, blue and yellow. When we read in a diary kept during the Civil War period in East Tennessee an old recipe for green, we realize this was a complicated art in itself.

> Take 4 parts of oil of vitriol to 1 of indigo. Mix it well in a bottle and shake it every 2 hours for 4 or 5 days. Then take a strong ooze of hickory bark and dissolve ½ lb. of alum to 3 or 4 gallons of ooze. Then put the vitriol and indigo in the alum mixture in small quantities until it is as deep as you like.

It was time-consuming and the results were often disappointing. Little wonder that many of the old recipe books concluded with a philosophical bit of advice, "Just suit your fancy." That is why cloth made in such circumstances was something to be cherished.

IV
The Quilt in America

While England by the early eighteenth century had succeeded in developing the making of quilts to a level of elegance, it was her colonists in the New World who turned this knack of needlecraft into a way of life that was to influence their whole cultural and social structure. It is significant that we find recorded in the Victoria and Albert Museum's *Notes on Applied Work and Patchwork,* "Patchwork of the eighteenth and nineteenth centuries arose independently in England and America."[1]

In looking back, we wonder with a sense of awe at the driving desire, as well as the persistence and ingenuity. It would seem nothing was too much trouble if it beautified—for instance, the transforming of a drab, rough-textured linsey-woolsey quilt into a brighter, more interesting article by glazing the whole surface with the whipped whites of eggs![2]

PLATE 14
Opposite: *Mary Jacquelin Quilt. This Virginia quilt, made during the second half of the eighteenth century, in some respects is similar to the earlier (1704) New England Saltonstall quilt (Plate 16). Both are made of silk materials in remarkably rich colors. The same technique of paperbacking as a foundation may have been used, but if so the paper has been removed from the Jacquelin quilt. Mary Jacquelin, believed to be the maker, was a descendant of Edward Jacquelin, one of the first emigrants to Jamestown, Virginia. The quilt is now in the John Marshall House, Richmond, Virginia.* Courtesy of the Association for the Preservation of Virginia Antiquities.

PLATE 15
Overleaf: *Saffron Satin Quilt. We do not know the exact house in Salem, Massachusetts, that was once graced by this luxurious quilt, but tradition says that it was on Salem's Washington Square and that there the Marquis de Lafayette slept under the quilt. The occasion, on October 29th, 1784, was one of much rejoicing and activity. According to the* Salem Annals, *"Multitudes of people rent the air with cheers of welcome." The striking color of the quilt may well have been achieved with safflower* (carthamus tinctorius), *an herb which produces large, vivid red and orange flowerheads. In directions for making dyes, it is often noted that "safflower can be used on silk." The quilt was presented, along with its traditional story, by Mrs. Edward Osgood to the Wenham Historical Association.* Courtesy of the Wenham Historical Association and Museum, Inc., Wenham, Massachusetts.

Of all the folk arts that testify to the industry and thrift of women in America, as well as to their desire for beauty and their determination to express that longing, the art of making patchwork quilts became the most universal. Other arts such as rug-making, weaving, embroidery, and stenciling were developed to a fine degree in this country. But it was the quilt that engaged the attention and devotion of women in all walks of life.

In their impressive mansions, each with its widow's walk from which they could scan the horizons hoping to sight a returning vessel, wives of rich New England sea captains passed long hours working on elaborate quilts, while waiting for adventurous husbands who roamed the seven seas. The wives gave such names as All Around the World, Lost Ship, and Ocean Wave to their quilts.

In the deep South, mistresses of gracious white-pillared plantation houses made exquisite quilts to adorn their massive four-posters, their workmanship as delicate as handmade lace. There was much visiting and social life in that part of the country, for the plantations were scattered some distance apart. In the days of dinners and balls, it was necessary for the guests to stay all night, so many bedrooms had to be available—as many as ten to twenty-five in some of the big houses.

In Charleston, South Carolina, in one year, 1768, there occurred twelve weddings among the wealthy residents of the city and all the furniture for these rich couples came from England. The twelve massive beds with canopies supported by heavily carved posts, decorated with rice stalks and full heads of grain, were so high that steps were needed in order

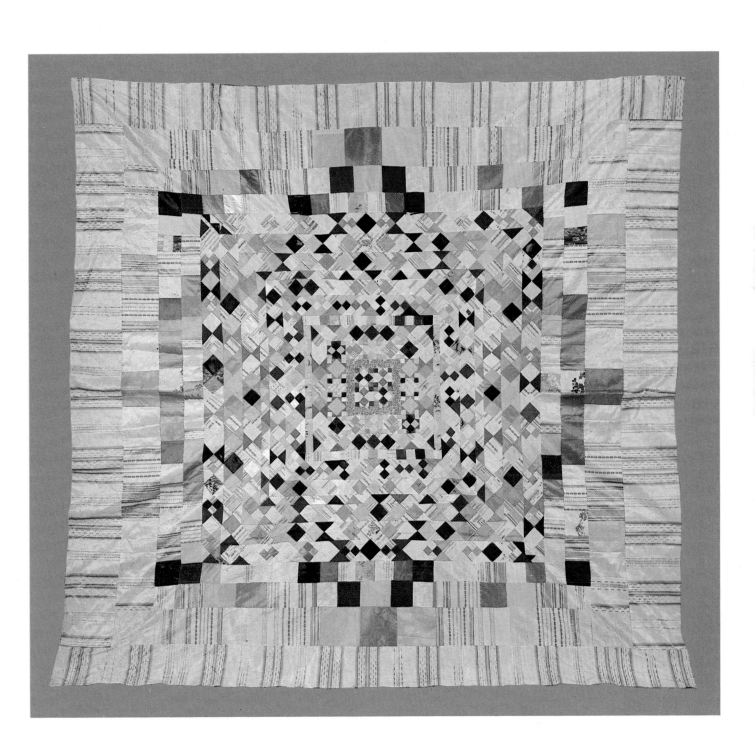

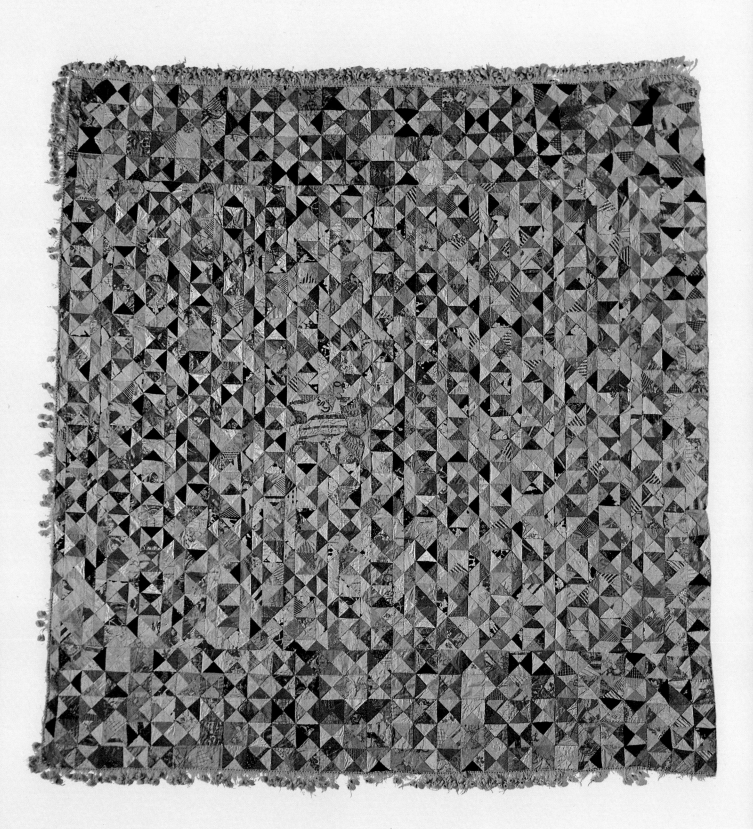

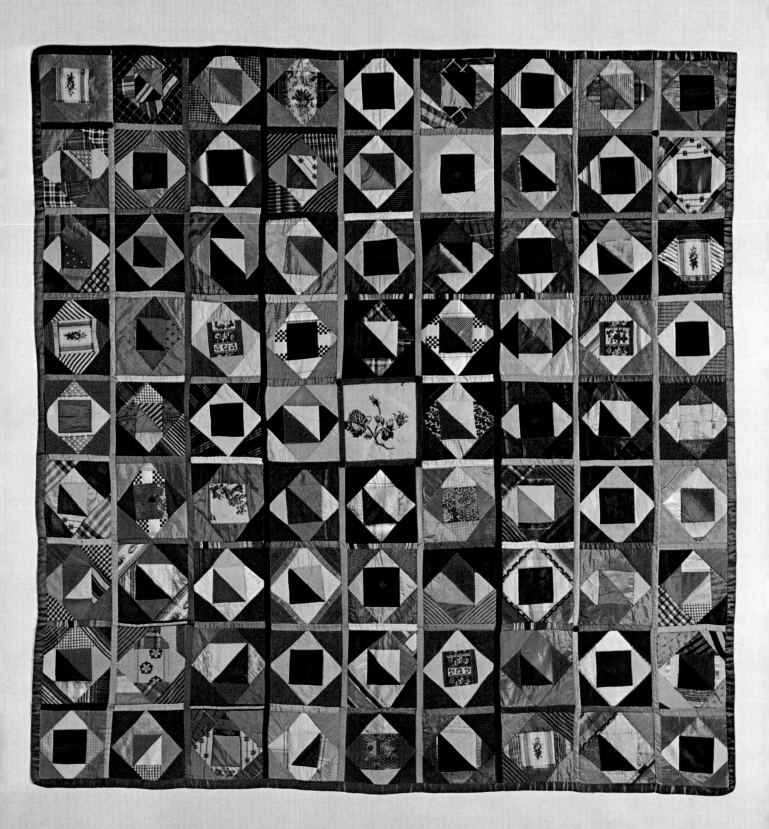

to climb into them. Elaborate curtains and spreads were furnished to correspond. In one early inventory, there are mentioned four feather beds, bolsters . . . one yellow mohair bed counterpane and two green silk quilts.[3]

To supply such luxurious bedcovering in the houses of the rich planters, it was only natural that the slaves were taught to do fine needlework and become proficient in the art of quiltmaking.

From old scrapbooks, inventories, and wills in every part of colonial America, we learn what was considered important. Among such prized possessions as "tea tables, looking glasses, pewter mugs, silver tankards, and spoons" to be passed on to dearly beloveds and cherished as the owners had cherished them, high on the list are "quilts, coverlids, and counterpanes." From such a document we learn that "before Captain Kidd turned pirate, he set up housekeeping in New York with his wife, Sarah, in 1692, and among the sixty items of household furnishings were three quilts, probably of Mrs. Kidd's wedding dowry."[4]

From its humble beginnings, the quilt had risen in the social scale. As early as 1716, quiltmaking had become a flourishing activity in Boston and was considered important enough for special instruction to be given in the art. The *Boston News Letter* carried in that year the following advertisement:

> This is to give Notice, that at the House of Mr. George Brownell, late School Master in Hanover Street Boston, are all sorts of Millinery Works done; . . . and also young Gentlewomen and Children taught all sorts of fine Works as Quilting, Feather-Work . . . Embroidering a new way, Turkey-Work for Handkerchiefs . . . flourishing and plain Work,

The Quilt in America

and Dancing cheaper than ever was taught in Boston, Brocaded Work for Handkerchiefs and short Aprons upon Muslin, artificial Flowers work'd with a Needle.

The *New England Journal* of March 20, 1727, advertises an auction of household goods at Sun Tavern in Dock Square, Boston. "Feather beds and quilts" were especially featured.

In October, 1729, when the "compleat furnishings" of the "mansion house and stables" of Governor Burnet were exposed to "Sale by Publick Vendue at the House wherein his late Excellency dwelt in Boston," "beds and bed curtains of 'Chintz,' quilts, and counterpanes" were included.

In the records of sales of the Fairfax estate at Belvoir, Virginia, there is included the item, "George Washington purchased 19 coverlids or quilts to take back home to Martha at Mt. Vernon."[5]

But it was not only in the more established centers or in the homes of the well-to-do that quiltmaking held the center of attention. Women isolated in mountain fastnesses up and down the Appalachian range and wives of obscure fishermen in New England coastal villages alike kept their fingers and minds busy "piecin' patches," and the quilts coming from their hands reflected the happenings in a new land.

One of the most fascinating features of American quilt lore, showing great imagination on the part of our ancestors, is that of the names given to the quilts. These names, sometimes called "folkloric poetry," were often inspired by familiar objects: a horseshoe, windmill, a tumbler, monkey wrench, the little red schoolhouse. History, religion, politics, humor, pathos, and tragedy are all there.

Events of historical significance can be traced in the evolution of quilt names. As Martha Genung Stearns says in *Homespun and Blue*, "The names of bed quilt patterns are some of the straws that showed how the wind was blowing."[6] There was Burgoyne Surrounded, a quilt worked out in dark blue rectangles said to be taken from an actual plan of the battle, regiments being represented on military plans as small black blocks. After we had won our Revolution and were no longer under British domination, it was natural that American quiltmakers preferred to call the once popular pattern, Queen Charlotte's Crown, by the name of Indian River.

Our forebears were very religious and many names held Biblical connotations. The old pattern Job's Tears became known as the Slave Chain in the 1800's when slavery was the paramount subject of the day and both men and women transferred their deep concern into social action. The same pattern later became Texas Tears when Texas was the topic of national interest. Still later it was rechristened the Endless Chain.

Wherever and whenever a path was broken, the quilt went along. It might be carried by the lone traveler who made his way by foot, his quilt rolled in a bundle under his arm, perhaps to be used as his bed or containing his few possessions. During that exciting period of our national expansion when the cry of "Westward Ho!" rang throughout the land, those fortunate enough to make their way westward in sturdy Conestoga wagons made sure that the quilt went along, not only as a necessary part of equipment but as a continuing part of their social structure.

The Quilt in America

As the caravans of covered wagons rolled across the plains, the old quilt patterns recorded their progress. The Carolina Rose became the Prairie Rose when it reached Western soil, and in Texas the Star of the East became the Texas Star or Lone Star. And what could speak more poignantly of the hardships these women braved than the names they gave their quilts: Rocky Road to Kansas, Crosses and Losses, Indian Hatchet, Texas Tears, Kansas Dugout.

Since the quilt served as an artistic expression of the maker, the name was rightfully whatever she chose. She might adhere to the traditional name given by a maker long ago, or it was her privilege to designate it by whatever she had in mind. Usually a name held some personal significance or sentimental meaning and the more imaginative she was, the more expressive it was apt to be.

The same quilt patterns might show up in various localities far removed from one another but known by different names. Ship's Wheel in Cape Cod might be called Harvest Sun in Pennsylvania farmlands or Hand of Friendship by their Quaker neighbors. A patch called Rocky Glen in the Appalachian Mountains might be Lost Ship on New England's rugged coast. The pattern known in New England in pre-Revolutionary days as Jacob's Ladder became Stepping Stones in Virginia, while in Benjamin Franklin's adopted Pennsylvania, it was known as the Tail of Benjamin's Kite.

The all-too-well-known Drunkard's Trail or Drunkard's Path may have been named by a village jokester; others would have preferred a more poetic name such

PLATE 18

Windmill. A familiar object abstracted into a complicated quilt pattern through the joining of triangles to form a four-patch. Other versions of the same design are Water Wheel, Mill Wheel, and Water Mill. Still other names are Corn and Peas, and Hour Glass. This quilt of many pieces is striking in dark blue and white. Laurenzi Collection.

as Wanderer's Path or Wonder of the World as more conducive to pleasant dreams.

Superstitions played a part in quilt names. Wandering Foot was unfortunately named since the wandering foot was supposed to have a malign influence. Mothers were careful not to let their children sleep under it for fear they would grow up to be discontented or of a roving disposition. For the same reason, no bride would have one in her hope chest. When the name was changed to Turkey Track the spell was broken. The same pattern developed in green and white is quite lovely and is called the Iris Leaf by some makers.

The old pattern, Bear's Paw, reflects in its name the dangers encountered in frontier living. In more settled communities, where bears had moved out but the roads were only mud trails, the same pattern was called Duck's Foot in the Mud. In Pennsylvania, the Friends called it the Hand of Friendship. The Pine Tree is one pattern that has supposedly kept the same name throughout the United States, probably because the pine tree is found from coast to coast.

It would be impossible to list all the names for quilt patterns; they are as diversified and as American as the art of patchwork itself, but some are recurrent and well known. Star names easily lead the list: Twinkling Star, Morning Star, Evening Star, Feathered Star, Shooting Star, Star of the East, Star of Bethlehem, Varied Star.

Rose names were extremely popular: California Rose, Mexican Rose, Moss Rose, Rose of Sharon, Harvest Rose, Whig Rose, Democratic Rose.

Some floral and poetic names were: Princess Feather, Woods in Autumn, Drooping Lily, Wind-blown Tulip.

Humorous names played a part: Crazy Ann, Old Maid's Dream, Bachelor's Puzzle, Shootin' Minnow, Wild Goose Chase.

The trades of the time were a source of inspiration: Anvil, Saw-tooth, Carpenter's Wheel, Watermill, Windmill, Dusty Miller, Churn Dash, Double Monkey Wrench.

Those suggested by recreation were few in comparison. Two suggested by the square dance are: Eight Hands Around, Swing in the Center.

Some of the names must have been used for children's quilts for the old-fashioned trundle bed: Four Little Birds, Goose in the Pond, Children's Delight, Toad in the Puddle, Johnny around the Corner, Ducks and Ducklings, House that Jack Built.

And of course many names from the Bible were used: Jacob's Coat, Solomon's Crown, Forbidden Fruit Trees, Robbing Peter to Pay Paul.

V
Stories About Quilts: Social, Romantic, Political

In our present-day world of easy transportation and almost instantaneous communication, it is hard to appreciate what it meant in a slower moving era to meet with friends and neighbors for the purpose of working together. Even the prospect of it afforded excitement and pleasure. In pioneer days it may have been to a great extent "every man for himself," yet those were the times when friends were most necessary and their help was readily given.

In looking back, writers of the present day are recognizing the significance of quilts. Edith and Harold Holzer state, "Their importance in the social development of the United States is becoming an acknowledged anthropological fact; no other art, the sociologists say, brought so many people together to work en masse; and no other art in the history of the world was so completely dominated by women."[1]

Even the "picking bees" became fun when neighbors

PLATE 19

Pineapple Log Cabin Design. A section is shown of this brilliantly colored version of the old basic Log Cabin design, done in cottons. The pattern has come a long way from its humble beginnings (such as Plate 10). Offen Collection.

76

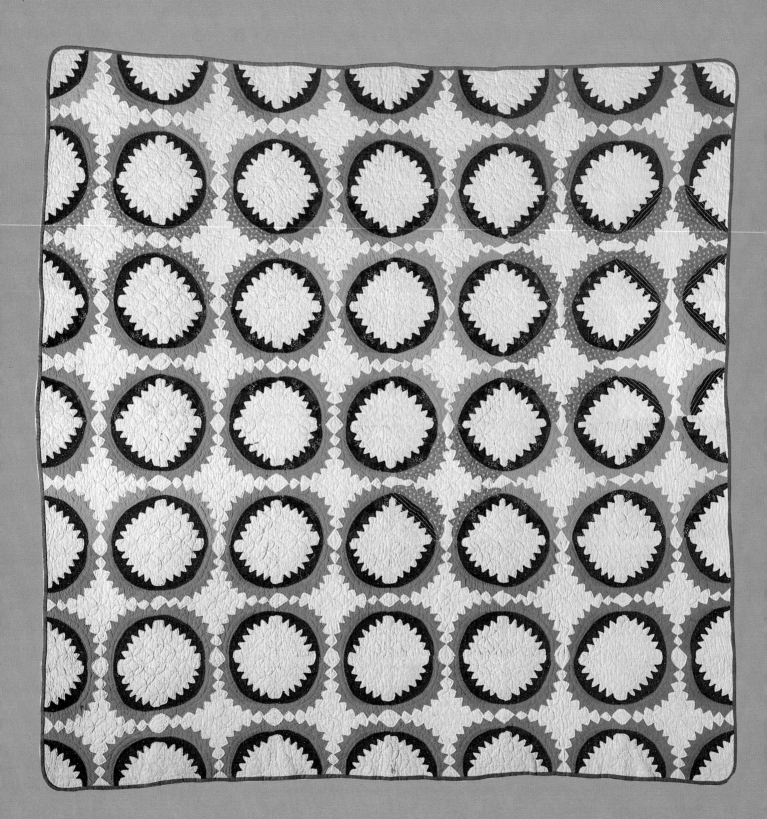

met to help one another in the cleansing and separating of tangled masses of wool in preparation for the carding and spinning that would follow. Husking bees, when the corn was stripped for winter storage, usually ended with square dancing. Apple-parings, logrollings, barn raisings, housewarmings were all welcome events that helped to break the monotony of lonely, routine hard work. And the quilt made its unique contribution. Of all the community gatherings, nothing could compare with the excitement of the quilting bee. As time went on, these became more and more social events—the really genteel parties, and no one wanted to be left out of a quilting! Alice Morse Earle writes of a quilting party in Narragansett in 1752 that lasted ten days.[2]

Taking its name from the busy honeymaker, a quilting bee was held for the purpose of quilting the finished quilt top which was stretched on a large quilting frame. If the size of the house would allow it, a number of frames, each with its quilt top in readiness, might be set up awaiting the expert hands of the quilters who would arrive in sleighs, wagons, or carriages if coming from a distance, while nearer friends arrived on foot.

Women of all ages vied to be among those asked to participate and, of course, good quilters were most sought after. As in earlier times in Europe, a girl had to become expert with her needle, able to compete with the older, more experienced quilters if she wanted to be a part of the real activity. Otherwise, she might be relegated to the culinary department to help prepare the food for supper, and would miss the fun of sitting around the frames where there was brighter chatter and gossip. Here, as the work pro-

PLATE 20

Stars Within Red, White, and Blue Circles. This intricate composition at first glance appears to be a pieced quilt, but upon examination one finds that the designs are actually appliquéd. The quilt top was made in Illinois, c. 1850, by Mrs. Owen Brown, the mother of John Brown, the Abolitionist. Mrs. Brown was engaged in the business of helping to outfit covered wagons going farther west. When a niece and her family were leaving Illinois for Sacramento, California (arriving there in 1851 according to family letters), Mrs. Brown gave her some quilts, including this unfinished quilt top. The niece happened also to be named Mrs. Brown, and it was her daughter who prized the quilt top and made it into the finished quilt, constructing the lining from commercial flour bags and doing the quilting herself. She would never allow the quilt to be used, hence its excellent condition. It is well documented. In time, this same daughter of Mrs. Brown gave the quilt to her own daughter, Kathryn Leslie, who came to Connecticut to live. The quilt later became the property of a friend, Paul Pickhardt, who in turn gave it to his sister, Mrs. Jere Coleman of Cambridge, Massachusetts. It was sold to the author in March, 1966. Bacon Collection.

Stories About Quilts

PLATE 21

Captain May in the Mexican War. The Museum notes for this vari-colored cotton appliqué quilt state, "Past owner has said this quilt from the Noll family, Montgomery County, Maryland, c. 1850, depicts in appliqué designs the mounted figure of Capt. May as he charged at the Battle of Reseca de La Palma, adapted from the lithograph by Nathaniel Currier showing Gen. Taylor at the Battle, Capt. May receiving orders to charge the Mexican Batteries, May 9, 1846." Courtesy of the Shelburne Museum, Shelburne, Vermont.

gressed and the quilt was rolled on its frame, the quilters were brought closer together so that there was a chance to exchange confidences and talk over the latest affairs of the heart. Trying to be the one to put in the tiniest stitches was tedious, but there was plenty of fun and interest to lighten the work. Being an accomplished needlewoman in those days was as much a social asset as being a good bridge player is today.

Having an important bee meant much planning on the part of the host and hostess—providing hitching and stable room for the horses and vehicles, cooking and baking in advance for the supper, shining the pewter and brass, having plenty of candles ready, and, of course, laying out the best quilts on the big four-posters. Then the hostess was ready to welcome the people of the countryside. The guests came early, got right to work, and stayed until all the quilt tops were completed. The menfolk, dressed in their best, joined the party for a bountiful supper, and the evening ended in a grand frolic of games, singing, dancing, and courting. No wonder that such an atmosphere inspired Stephen Foster to compose his beloved song, "Aunt Dinah's Quilting Party," and no wonder that the young man got his nerve to pop the question as he was "Seeing Nellie Home."

An invitation to a quilting was welcome at any time, but it is easy to imagine how especially welcome it would have been, coming after a long, hard winter. An old letter, written in Ohio and dated February 7, 1841, reads:

We have had deep snow. No teams passed for three weeks but as soon as the drifts could be broken

through, Mary Scott sent her boy Frank around to say she was going to have a quilting.[3]

Often a quilting was the occasion for a young lady to announce her engagement, and her hope-chest quilts would be quilted. A girl usually did not quilt her quilt tops until she was reasonably certain of marriage, for it meant a real outlay of money to provide the cloth for the linings and the filling for the interlinings of her dozen or so quilts. "The quilting was in those days considered the most solemn and important recognition of a betrothal."[4]

In writing of such an affair, Thomas Hamilton Ormsbee tells of the significance of the heart design used in connection with the quilts of a prospective bride, and many stories have come down to us relative to that very special quilt called the Bride's Quilt. The stories are much the same in essence. Most agree that it was supposed to be made by the bride-to-be, whether it was made during the years before she became engaged with the hope of marriage in mind, or made nearer the wedding date—the very last of her hope-chest quilt tops to be finished. Mr. Ormsbee says:

> The [quilt] top might have been made years before and folded away in the dower chest. But invitations to a quilting where the heart design was employed was tantamount to an engagement announcement. For hearts were the insignia of a bride and up until 1840 such a design used in any quilt other than that of a bride was considered unlucky and presaged that dire disaster of a broken engagement.[5]

Perhaps no form of folk art ever developed into a greater "hearts and flowers" affair than the patchwork quilt in America. From its practical and prosaic beginnings, it became interwoven with romance until it fairly dripped with sentiment.

The quilting bees were one of the few social diversions outside the church, ranking high in popularity with the church socials and the box suppers. Here the background for romance was provided, the bee serving as a kind of matrimonial bureau for all ages.

Little girls were brought up on stories of hope-chest quilts and bride's quilts and, just as they did their daily "stents" on their samplers (for "idle hands were the devil's work tools"), they learned early to work on their quilt squares. No doubt the samplers with their pious mottoes and carefully worked alphabets were more edifying, but the making of a quilt square could be more exciting. It just *might* develop into a Bride's Quilt! There are records of little girls starting their bride's quilts at the tender ages of eight and nine years.

That Bride's Quilt! In this day of mass production and machine-made articles, it's quite staggering to consider the thought, time, and effort that went into its making. The choice of the pattern alone was of great moment. Many carried variations of the heart motif, such as hands-over-hearts or hearts in a four-leaf clover arrangement. Other sentimental designs included Lovers' Knots, Linked Wedding Rings, Love Rose, Cupid's Arrowpoints, and Crescent Moon, signifying virginity. Looking forward to a long life together, the couple might decide upon a variation of Oak Leaves, a pattern foretelling longevity.

Often the young man involved would help his young lady work out the design for the quilt and also the pattern for the quilting. We can imagine their choosing some favorite flower as they courted in the old-fashioned garden.

The main difference in the stories pertaining to the Bride's Quilt seems to be in the number of quilts required to make up a proper dowry. Some say that there should be twelve in the dowry and that the thirteenth, the bride's very own, brought the number up to the thirteen of a "baker's dozen." Others claim that the number of dowry quilts need be only twelve, starting with the goodly number of ten which could be made by the bride, her mother, or her friends. To these, the bride-to-be added hers, of course made by her own hands. Then, at the time of marriage, a twelfth quilt, a Freedom Quilt, was added by the bridegroom, thus completing the good round dozen.

A Freedom Quilt rivaled the Bride's Quilt in significance, and there is much fascinating lore connected with it. Much was made of a young man's coming of age. Custom decreed that he be given a new suit of clothes called a Freedom Suit, and in like manner it was considered appropriate that he be given a Freedom Quilt, which could be made by his mother, sister, or friends. If marriage was not imminent, his quilt was carefully laid away until the time when he decided to marry. Freedom quilts were apt to be developed in red, white, and blue, often depicting crossed flags, emblazoned eagles, stars and stripes, or some other masculine or patriotic theme.

In Mrs. Ruth Finley's *Old Patchwork Quilts and the Women Who Made Them,* there is a charming account of the commemoration of a boy's twenty-first birthday:

> In the old days a youth's arrival at years of legal discretion was an important event. No longer could

his parents or guardian bind him out as an apprentice, take his wages, make him work at home for nothing, or legally restrain his actions in any way. He was *free*. Wealthy parents, copying the time-honored custom of England as observed, especially in the case of the eldest son, made of a boy's twenty-first birthday an affair of great display. In families of more modest income, an evening "company" was the order of the day, in honor of which occasion the young man wore his "freedom suit." Even bound boys were given a new suit of clothes by the master from whose service their twenty-first birthday released them.[6]

A Bride's Quilt or a Freedom Quilt is an heirloom to be cherished, and fortunately there still exist outstanding examples of each. I had the good fortune to be the recipient of a most unusual and attractive quilt, which may have been intended to become a Freedom Quilt. It fits into that category in some ways. But I prefer to call it a Bridegroom's Quilt because of the provocative story which was given to me with the quilt by a direct descendant of the popular bridegroom for whom it was made.

The young man was Henry Thompson Leighton of Blackstrap, Maine, and what a catch he must have been considered! Each of its gay blocks, all fashioned from pink calico prints, was by a different girl friend, and the heart design, the motif supposedly reserved for a Bride's Quilt, is featured in many of the carefully wrought squares. Did all the makers of those romantic squares hope or expect to be the lucky girl? Certainly this was true of one ardent admirer who signed herself "Poppy" in a letter written to Henry in 1867. We can judge the emotional state she had reached as she writes from "Land of Paradise / 67":

My dear Henry,

Would that my tongue could utter or my pen express that amount of *undying* affection which my heart pours out for you. "Would I were with you every day and hour" that I might minister to thy happiness, thou sweet one. Why will you remain so unmoved by my loving looks and acts? Can I forget thee? *Never* while my spirit haunts this mortal frame. Thou divine effulgence of beauty, how can I say enough in thy praise? When I reflect on thy many good qualities how my heart thrills with rapture in thinking "he may yet be *mine*."

O! my pride when you read this will it not seem to you, you are reading the first outpourings of a heart young in years but O! so old in affection. Will it not strike you that we are kindred spirits created for each other and some plan in this mighty universe will remain unfinished if we are not at last united in the "holy bonds of matrimony"?

Farewell and may this be only the beginning of a friendship which shall never terminate this side of the grave.

"Thine-ever
Poppy"

It was beautiful Maria Josephine Bateman (named for two queens), not Poppy, who succeeded in capturing the wily Henry. Let us hope she did not mind too much any previous romances. Certainly her mother-in-law, who set the blocks together at the time of her son's marriage to Maria Josephine, was a wise and politic lady. Amid all the pink romantic blocks, in the very center of the quilt top, she carefully featured in large, appliquéd letters the word FRIENDSHIP. (Plate 23.)

But it was not only romance, gossip, and small talk that held the attention of the ladies who made quilts and attended the quilting parties. With few

PLATE 22
Cape Cod Bridal Quilt. An unusually handsome bridal quilt from Osterville, Massachusetts. The design is deep red appliqué Oak Leaf on a white background. Made between 1803 and 1810, it is impressive in size, design, and workmanship and has on each side a stunning, very wide border in exquisite trapunto. Offen Collection.

Stories About Quilts

newspapers to circulate current events, here was the chance to learn the latest bits of news. Ideas, too, were exchanged, and it can be safely said that the quiltings were the forerunners of today's women's clubs. Many a quilt name bears testimony that our foremothers took an interest in the changing social and political scenes: White House Steps, Lincoln's Platform, Slave Chain, Confederate Rose, Dolley Madison's Star, Rose of Dixie, Whig Rose, Mexican Rose, Democratic Rose, Old Tippecanoe, Clay's Choice, Mrs. Cleveland's Choice.

Much of the talk was good talk. Not only did they discuss their quilts and the concocting of dyes for their materials, but many subjects of general interest. In Harriet Beecher Stowe's novel, *The Minister's Wooing*, she gives a detailed account of a quilting supposed to have taken place in a seafaring New England village about 1800:

> The conversation never flagged, ranging from theology to recipes of corn fritters, sly allusions to the future "lady of the parish" to the doctrine of free will and predestination.[7]

As the women expanded their thinking, the quiltings took on a significance that was of great moment. A new movement was stirring and the idea of Women's Rights was taking root. By the 1850's, women were giving time and effort to causes such as antislavery and temperance, and naturally these were heatedly discussed around the quilting frames. Susan Brownell Anthony, zealous advocate of complete equality for the sexes, delivered her first talk on "Equal Rights" at a church quilting party held in Cleveland, Ohio. A militant forerunner of Women's Lib, by 1868 Miss Anthony was proprietor of a weekly paper called *The Revolution,* its motto being: "The true Republic—men, their rights and nothing more; women, their rights and nothing less."

A historic piece of patchwork in the form of our American flag was produced at a quilting party, its stripes being pieced together and its stars applied. It was made by the girls of Portsmouth, New Hampshire, according to specifications given them by the dashing young hero of the day, Captain John Paul Jones, founder of the American Navy. Composed of red and white slices from their best gowns, this silken flag that flew on the *Ranger*, July 7, 1777, was the first edition of the Stars and Stripes Europe ever saw. And the white stars shining against the bright blue field of the "unconquered flag" had been cut from a cherished bridal gown, the gown of Helen Seavey, wedded in May, 1777, to a young officer of the New Hampshire line. Of the ladies of the quilting party who made the flag, only five names are now known— Mary Langdon, Caroline Chandler, Helen Seavey, Augusta Pierce, and Dorothy Hall (niece of Elijah Hall, second lieutenant on the *Ranger*).[8]

A stirring account recalling the history of that flag was given in a speech made by Commodore Jones on November 29, 1781, at the Town Hall in Portsmouth:

> A flag was made for that ship [the *Ranger*], by the dainty hands of Portsmouth's daughters, of a pattern new to the world. That flag the *Ranger* carried across the sea and showed alike to our French friends and our English enemies. The story of that flag has been written in letters of blood and flame that can never be rubbed out so long as Liberty shall be the watchword of brave men and virtuous women.[9]

We have, as if one great family, a common heritage

Stories About Quilts

in the American quilt and its homespun lore. We only wish we could read between the tiny stitches, for in every quilt there lies a story. Today, as these treasures are rediscovered and displayed, they become objects of pride, the old patterns blending surprisingly well with contemporary decor.

Perhaps, though, because of the very familiarity of the quilt in the lives of generations not too far removed, there is often very little known of the important role it played. This can be true of the things nearest us and may account for a reply given a bit disdainfully by a lady when asked what she knew about quilts, "Quilts? Why, quilts are just quilts, that's all." But, as she looked at my quilts, she seemed to become interested in spite of herself. Memories of her childhood began coming back to her and one quilt seemed to evoke something especially haunting. Amazingly, on two of the white squares at the top of the quilt which covered the pillows, there had been embroidered in bright red the loving, little messages to herself and her twin sister, "Good Night and Good Morning—Winona and Bertha," respectively.

Surviving as proof of the high state of development of the quilt in New England as early as the 1700's is a wonderfully wrought quilt belonging to the famous Saltonstall family. (Plate 16.) It was made by a member or members of the family of John Leverett, Deputy Governor of the Massachusetts Bay Colony, re-elected to the office five consecutive times before his death in 1678. In all probability, it was made around 1704 by his widow Sarah (Sedgwick) Leverett with the aid of his daughter Elizabeth (who became Mrs. Elisha Cooke in 1668). It descended through the Leverett family to the Saltonstall family, and

PLATE 23

Friendship Quilt. Made for Henry Thompson Leighton of Blackstrap, Maine. After he had married the beautiful Maria Josephine Bateman, it became a "Bridegroom's Quilt." It contains more than forty pink appliquéd squares, each square made by a different young woman! Henry's politic mother set the sentimental squares together and appliquéd the word Friendship in the center. Bacon Collection.

its present owner, the Honorable Leverett Saltonstall, a former United States senator from Massachusetts, is a direct descendant of the maker. Family tradition says that through the succeeding generations, the quilt was used on the "state beds." This, of course, may have meant the most important beds, but also it could mean just what the tradition says, "state beds," for there have been many distinguished statesmen in both the Leverett and Saltonstall families.

Besides having a background of such unusual interest and distinction, it is a gem of a coverlet and a fine example of early American needlecraft. A pieced quilt, it is composed of fine bits of silks, brocades, and velvets, set together in a design which can assume the forms of a square, diamond, star, bow tie, hourglass, even a windmill, depending upon the angle one looks at it. It is not a quilted coverlet and probably was intended to be only decorative. It has a lining which is of much later material, but no interlining. It boasts a handsome three-inch border of handmade fringe and measures two yards three inches by two yards ten inches.

A most unusual feature, and rather amusing on so handsome a quilt, is the appliquéd angel that adorns the center of the quilt. Appliquéd on top of the silk-and-brocade-pieced pattern, it would appear that this was an afterthought, added perhaps many years after the original was finished. Although the effect is a bit like gilding the lily, it certainly adds interest.

From a historic point of view, the Saltonstall quilt holds unusual significance. While we gain an indication of the period in which it was made from the scraps of silks and brocades themselves, even more indicative of the time element are the bits of paper over which each bit of cloth was first basted before being sewed together and which had been left within the quilt.[10] When Samuel Eliot Morison, noted Harvard historian, examined the quilt in the early 1930's, he discovered that many of these bits of paper had been cut from a Harvard College catalog of 1701, only one copy of which, owned by the college, was known to be in existence. He carefully removed some of the bits of paper and pasted them together and presented them to Leverett Saltonstall, who was then the governor of the Commonwealth of Massachusetts.

Many a New England quilt shows the influence of strange lands brought by clipper ships when the masters of the great vessels carried home priceless treasures. "Those tall ships which shuttled back and forth across the world wove many strange strands into the fabric of New England," writes Martha Genung Stearns.[11] A striking example of this era is the Tree of Life quilt in the Atkinson-Lancaster Collection of the New England Historic and Genealogical Society in Boston.[12] The quilt was developed from a handpainted calico bedspread of unusual beauty, from India, which had been purchased by Captain Caleb Cook, Sr., of Salem, probably between 1798 and 1800.

Another Massachusetts quilt of historic interest, composed of choice silks, satins, and brocades, boasts in its center a piece of the brocade gown which Sally Crowninshield wore when she danced with President George Washington in Salem back in 1789. (Plate 17.)

As a memento of Rachel Ball's flower-sprigged yellow calico dress, which she wore in 1782 in Newark, New Jersey, when she danced with General Lafayette, there remains only a cherished tiny quilt square to tell the story. And when someone exclaims

PLATE 24

Bidwell Family Autograph Quilt. This outstanding quilt is a genea- logical record of the Bidwell family of Elmira, New York, and Monterey, Massachusetts. A most unusual feature connected with it is the existence of a watercolor chart, executed with the minutest care, which served as a guide for the making of the quilt. The twenty-six squares were made by various members of the Bidwell family and each contains a signature lettered in India ink and a number corresponding to a numbered square on the chart. The hand-painted chart, dated 1859, depicts the design of each square, and on the reverse side are written the names of the individuals who fashioned them and the dates when they finished their work. Laurenzi Collection.

"What? A ball gown of calico—not silk?" we are re- minded of times of crisis in our national history when good cotton cloth was a precious commodity indeed. And Ruth E. Finley states that "fine calicoes were used for ball gowns as late as 1840."

In California and Oregon, lovingly preserved by descendants of the makers, are quilts that made the tortuous trip across country when the caravans of covered wagons rolled westward. Equally cherished and significant are quilts that were made on lonely plains, copied from remembered quilts back home by women who felt that quiltmaking somehow served as a tie with the past and perhaps the last link with a way of life left far behind.

A quilt made by Elizabeth B. Welch in 1848 tells a story of the Gold Rush era, a young wife and mother with a three-year-old girl, who stayed at home and worked in a textile mill in Lowell, Massachusetts, while her husband, Samuel Reed Welch, went to California to bring back fame and fortune. While he was gone, she used her meager savings to purchase print cloth and pieced together a Rising Sun quilt as a welcome-home gift. At last, a letter came saying he was on his way home and that he had been "more fortunate than other men, finding more gold than any others. You will never have to work again." He was to travel home by way of the Isthmus of Panama and she and the little girl were to meet him at a board- ing house in Boston on a stipulated date. But there she was met by two strangers who gave her a large chamois-skin pouch that appeared to have been full at one time but now contained only a sprinkling of gold dust and half a dozen small nuggets. Her hus- band, they said, had been taken ill at the Isthmus and

Job praying for his enemies. Jobs crosses. Jobs coffin.	The dark day of May, 19, 1780. The seven stars were seen 12. N. in the day. The cattle all went to bed, chickens to roost and the trumpet was blown. The sun went off to a small spot and then to darkness.	The serpent lifted up by Mosses and women bringing their children to look upon it to be healed.
Jonah casted over board of the ship and swallowed by a whale. Turtles.	God created two of every kind, Male and female	The falling of the stars on Nov. 13, 1833. The people were frighten and thought that the end of time had come. God's hand staid the stars. The varmints rushed out of their beds.
Cold Thursday, 10. of Feb. 1895. A woman frozen while at prayer. A woman frozen at a gateway. A man with a sack of meal frozen. Isicles formed from the breath of a mule. All blue birds killed. A man frozen at his jug of liquor.	The red light night of 1846. A man tolling the bell to notify the people of the wonder. Women, children and fowls frightened but Gods merciful hand caused no harm to them.	Rich people who were taught nothing of God. Bob Johnson and Kate Bell of Virginia. They told their parents to stop the clock at one and to morrow it would strike one and so it did. This was the signal that they entered everlasting punishment. The independent hog which ran 500 miles from Ga. to Va. her name was Betts.
Adam and Eve in the garden. Eve tempted by the serpent. Adam's rib by with which Eve was made. The sun and moon. God's all seeing eye and God's merciful hand.	Two of every kind of animals continued. camels, elephants, "gheraffs" lions, etc.	The creation of animals continues.
John baptising Christ and the spirit of God descending and rested upon his shoulder like a dove.	The angels of wrath and the seven vials. The blood of fornications. Seven headed beast and 10 horns which arose out of the water.	The crucifixtion of Christ between the two thieves. The sun went into darkness. Mary and Martha weeping at his feet. The blood and water run from his right side.

PLATE 25
Harriet Powers Quilt— Biblical Scenes. This striking quilt, worthy of a Matisse, seems at first glance modern in concept and sophistication of design. It was made by a black woman in Athens, Georgia, probably between 1895 and 1898. A similar quilt made by Mrs. Powers is now in the Smithsonian Institution. Descriptive captions were written by Mrs. Powers. Courtesy of the Boston Museum of Fine Arts.

they had nursed him, but he had died and they had buried him there. The quilt was folded up and laid away, and some eighty years later the story was told to the grandchildren in the Hildreth family in Marblehead Neck, Massachusetts.

A quilt that made the trip from Tennessee to Texas and back again tells another story, as recounted to me by Mrs. James Dilworth, a charming ninety-year-old lady who still spoke of the Civil War as the "un-Civil War." Mrs. Dilworth had a remarkable memory and loved to show her cherished quilts, made during the prosperous period in the South when they were considered a pastime and much work was lavished upon them. She told of a quilt from the old haunted house that had stood on the Biltmore estate in Asheville, North Carolina, made by the girl-bride who had come over the mountains from Culpepper County, Virginia. Amazingly, before each of the tiny one-half-inch-square pieces had been sewn together, she had whipped over the ravelings of each one. When I remarked about the time and effort that had gone into such an operation, she said, "But, after all, it was real ladies' work."

Another quilt had been made by Mrs. Dilworth's mother, Mrs. Phoebe Drake Horton (b. 1810). It is signed "P.D.H. July 7, 1832" and is a fine example of the period of quiltmaking when the appliqué patterns were cut out from chintz and applied on fine white cambric. Hers was done with beautiful designs of pheasants, combining rich colors of old blues and browns.

Her greatest treasure, however, was the pieced silk quilt of the Pineapple design which had made the

PLATE 26
Sampler Quilt, Pieced and Appliquéd. Not even the most ambitious quiltmaker could hope to make a quilt of every design she admired, so she contented herself with collecting the patterns. Here the quiltmaker combined the two methods of patchwork. The central pieced motif is a cleverly blended pieced star in colors ranging from blue and red to yellow and brown, surrounded by eight large squares of appliqué designs. These include the pomegranate, oak leaf, tulip, and rose wreath—all set together with a Persian swirled print in tan and white. The tan and white calico lining is printed with the "Persian bear" or "pickle" pattern, copied from East India prints. Courtesy of the Friends of the Jackson Homestead Historical Museum, Newton, Massachusetts.

round trip from Tennessee to Texas. Tennessee was divided politically during the war, and many fortunes were lost. A great many Tennesseeans sought Texas as a place to recoup, and among them were the Dilworths from Jonesboro, Tennessee. Mrs. Dilworth had been a belle in her day, and the Pineapple Quilt contained scraps of dresses she had worn at inaugural balls and other functions in the Lone Star State, each one holding a story.

I remarked, "Didn't you have a good time?" and her response came quickly, "The best that was going."

Every aspect of life in America and abroad was reflected in quiltmaking. When Charles Dickens in his novel, *Barnaby Rudge,* created the bewitching Dolly Varden, she became a symbol. Among other things, a croquet game was named in her honor and, of course, a quilt pattern. Mrs. Robert D. Chellis of Wellesley owns a beautiful Dolly Varden quilt of graceful design.

A quilt from the South evokes nightmarish memories of the War Between the States and the flight of a family before the path of Sherman's army on its march to the sea. It bears forever the stains of mud spattered upon it as it served to cover the frightened children on the frantic drive over Georgia's red clay roads, as the family attempted to escape.

In the Boston Museum of Fine Arts is a Bride's Quilt of that same period, holding sad memories, carrying the significant date of 1860. It is of fine workmanship, an appliquéd quilt done in the Tulip design. It carries within its bordered edge a fine piping, often seen in the English quilts. This is the only example of such a treatment that I have noted in an American quilt.

The quilt was made by Miss Mary Cunningham of Danville, Kentucky, whose fiancé was killed early in the conflict. It was left in her will to her great-niece, Mrs. Samuel D. Wonders of Peterborough, New Hampshire, who presented it to the museum.

The Civil War and the bloody disputes over Kansas Territory are vividly brought to mind by a quilt top fashioned by the hands of John Brown's mother. It carries a threaded needle, fastened and rusted, in one of the tiny pieces. John was an eight-year-old boy when his mother died, and we wonder what fond hopes were stitched within the red, white, and blue blocks for the son who was to meet his tragic fate many years later at Harpers Ferry, Virginia (Plate 20).

It seems a far cry from the execution of John Brown at Harpers Ferry to beautiful Hawaii. But the subject of American quilts is all-encompassing, and certainly the story of the quilts that have come from our newest state is one of the most fascinating on record. It has been told in a number of books and periodicals, but it is so interesting it bears repeating.

The art of quiltmaking is a comparatively old one in Hawaii, and its story is a fascinating one. Quilts have played an important role in the life of the Islanders since March 31, 1820, when the brig *Thaddeus*, with the first American missionaries aboard, one hundred sixty-five days out of Boston, sailing along Hawaii's coast toward Kailua, dropped anchor at Kohala. Their mission was to bring the Bible to the natives for the nourishment of their souls, and the Mother Hubbard (muu-muu) for the covering of their bodies. Somehow they must have thought that sewing, specifically the making of quilts, would be good for both souls and bodies and, armed with scrap bags, they immedi-

ately introduced this art. In their zeal, they did not wait to get settled. Four royal ladies were picked up and brought aboard the *Thaddeus*. These were Kalukua, the queen dowager and mother of the young King Liholiho; Namahana, the king's aunt; and two wives of Chief Kalanimoku. On Monday morning, April 3, 1820, the American Board of Missions held its first sewing circle meeting with the royal ladies as its guests. There were eleven ladies present in all, and it must have presented a strange picture: the seven young matrons, wives of the missionaries, dressed in their small-waisted, tight-sleeved garments, their ankles discreetly hidden beneath billowy skirts, entertaining and instructing the Hawaiian ladies, their ample figures wrapped in folds of tapa from waist to below the knees, their brown bosoms and shoulders bare.[13]

The four women of rank were furnished with calico patchwork to sew and were given their first lesson in plying the scissors and running a needle, a "new employment to them." Whether the patchwork started that day ever developed into a quilt is not recorded. Perhaps the missionary ladies decided it was more important to get the bosoms and shoulders covered before going further with quilts.

Like most Polynesian people, the Hawaiians were fastidious about their bedding. They were already skilled in the handling of the inner wet bark of the *wauke* (mulberry) plant and shaping it into sheets of tapa of uniform size and thickness for use on their beds. They were accustomed to decorating these sheets with intricate original designs stamped or blocked with native dyes. This new idea of making cloth quilts appealed to them, and from this there developed a

PLATE 27
Hawaiian Monstera Pattern. A spectacular early quilt in green and white. The date is not known but an indication of age may be that the quilt is interlined with the feathers from the nene goose. It became illegal to kill this bird in the 1800's, when it was declared an endangered species. Also, the workmanship is inferior to that of later Hawaiian quilts. Courtesy of Julianne Puakalehuanani Bird.

Stories About Quilts

PLATE 28
Opposite: *Hawaiian Flag Quilt.*
This design is said to derive from
the Governor Farrington flag
designed c. 1806 by the English
sea captain George C. Beckley.
In 1898, when it became known
that Hawaii was to become
a Territory of the United States,
the ladies of the Islands, fearing
that their native emblems might
not be held in proper esteem,
went into a flurry of patriotic
quiltmaking. The traditional story
is that twenty quilts were made,
each with some variations but all
featuring the Royal Coat of Arms,
the Union Jack, and eight red,
white, and blue stripes signifying
the eight Islands. Ten of the
original twenty quilts are thought
to remain, of which this is one.
Courtesy of Julianne
Puakalehuanani Bird.

PLATE 29
Overleaf: *Hawaiian Akaka*
Waterfalls. An outstanding
example of the "scissors" art of
quiltmaking as it developed in
Hawaii. Not only is the overall
central design cut from one piece
of cloth and appliquéd, but the
intricate border is also cut from
one piece. The quilt is a companion
piece to the Breadfruit quilt
(Plate 30) made for Mrs. Paul
Toms, wife of the Reverend Paul
Toms. When in 1961 they were
leaving the Island to return to
America, the ladies of their church
set about making the elaborate
Breadfruit pattern for Mrs. Toms.
Time being too short for them to
make a quilt for Mr. Toms as
well, they commissioned the ladies
of the nearby Mormon Church to
fashion this beautiful Akaka
Waterfalls quilt for him. Courtesy
of the Reverend Paul Toms.

glorious product, the Hawaiian quilt. It differs entirely from the American pieced quilt. Having no scraps left over from making dresses, the Hawaiian women resisted the idea of cutting up material and sewing it back together. They devised another scheme that resulted in a type of quiltmaking that might be called "scissors' art." It fits into the category of patchwork appliqué in that the design, cut from one fabric, is applied on another. Two very large pieces of cloth, one white and one colored, are used. One must be large enough to cover the bed; usually this is a bed sheet. The colored cloth which is to comprise the design is folded in many layers. Then the design is cut out in the same manner as one cuts out a paper snowflake. The colored design is then opened, spread out, and pinned on the white fabric. The edges of the whole design are turned under and basted before being sewn with a whipping stitch.

There is no quick method of making a Hawaiian quilt—it requires imagination, deftness, and skill. "The average person takes from six months to several years to complete a quilt, which requires about one thousand hours of hand sewing." Beautiful quilts called *tifaifai*[14] (or *tikaikai*–Polynesian) have imaginative designs incorporating the native fruits and flowers of the islands. The national emblems make popular designs as well, while the names given to the quilts are as fascinating as the quilts themselves. Often there seems to be no connection between name and quilt, the quiltmaker keeping her meaning secret. Perhaps the ladies of Hawaii did not wish to adhere to established customs and purposely gave their quilts names foreign to the subjects. A certain code of ethics pre-

vails. The originator of a design considers the name her own, not to be used indiscriminately. Certainly it adds to the mystery of the quilt.

Sally McCracken writes, "To establish her claim to her creation, the designer finished her quilt before showing it off . . . Hawaiians often kept their quilt patterns in a hidden place . . . Much like the tartans of the Scottish clans, quilt patterns used to be exclusive to one family . . . heirlooms passed from one Hawaiian grandmother to the next generation. Every girl and boy was expected to bring at least one quilt to the marriage bed. Innovations in design, material, and techniques were assimilated and adapted in typical Hawaiian fashion. Just as nails introduced by the New England missionaries became fishing hooks, and hymns turned into hulas, so the prim patchwork quilt was transformed. Just as their ancestors with their eye for beauty and poetic imagery brought the world-wide craft of Kapa-making to its highest development in Hawaii, so new-era-Polynesians have transformed sewing of appliquéd quilts into an indigenous folk art."[15]

Some of these mysterious names are sheer poetry, even when translated—"round ball of lehus blossoms," "the rain that makes noise on the house," "wind that steals the love from Maui," and, the loveliest of all, "wind that wafts love from one to another."

PLATE 30
Previous page: *Hawaiian Bread-fruit Plant. Made in Hawaii in 1961 for Mrs. Paul Toms, lover of and authority on Hawaiian art. Hawaiian women developed an art in quiltmaking all their own, very different from the pieced quilt of the mainland. The whole design for this Breadfruit quilt is cut from one large piece of cloth and then appliquéd. Mrs. Toms says of her quilt, "It took five women three months to cut out and appliqué the design and another three months to quilt it. And this meant continuous working most of the days." A companion quilt is shown on Plate 29. Courtesy of Mrs. Paul Toms.*

PLATE 31
Opposite: *George Washington's Plumes. A Tennessee quilt of the early 1800's, English-inspired. The pattern may seem rather grandiose for the locale of east Tennessee, but George Washington was still the great hero, dear to those who had left their homes in the Wautauga Settlement (which would later become Tennessee) to help win the Battle of King's Mountain at a time when the fortunes of the Colonies were at their lowest ebb. This quilt has its practical side. Evidently, it was made for a bed that would stand in the corner of the room, perhaps the living room. Since on the back and far side none of the border motif would show, it was done to be seen and admired only on one side and across the foot of the bed. Bacon Collection.*

Stories About Quilts

VI
Victorian Quilt Mania and Decline

As time went on and the resources of the new country continued to expand, many women were relieved of their more arduous tasks and this gave more free time for quiltmaking. Although the quilt might still serve its original purpose of providing warmth, it had left its humble beginnings far behind. Great stress was placed upon its decorative qualities and, through the pursuance of these, a more affluent picture of America emerges.

In the world of textiles there became available a fascinating array of materials from which to choose, the names of many only memories today—calimanco, India "chinces," painted cambric, pealong, bombazine, zephyr, polished calico, toile de Jouy and the very important copperplate.[1] This, in spite of England's long war on the importation of cotton from India in order to protect her woolen industry and all the legislative measures connected with it. Flowered calicoes, which the women adored, were bootlegged for years in both England and America. But in the end the ladies' "Passions for fashions" won.[2]

The manufacturing of cloth in our own country was developing at a rapid pace, so that for a large number of women it was no longer necessary to weave their own.

Cloth, however, was still looked upon with great respect. Quiltmakers could not easily forget the strict embargoes and heavy taxes placed on them for the use of certain fabrics, especially the cotton prints from Calcutta. Nor could they forget the tedious and back-breaking hours spent at the loom in former days. So, the scrap bag remained one of the most prized items in every household, and neighbors delighted in swapping interesting bits of rare materials.

Quilts made the news. The almanacs of the 1800's carried quilt patterns for the benefit of their lady readers. Itinerant peddlers carried quilt patterns as stock-in-trade to be able to give their customers the very latest. This may account for identical patterns becoming popular in widely separated sections of the country.

Quilters developed a jargon of their own, which was as clear to them as certain expressions are to us today. While our ancestors would not have known what it was to "tune in," they would have understood perfectly a neighbor's remark when she said, "I put in today." This meant that her quilt top was finished and had been put in the quilt frame to be quilted.

Not all quilts waited for a party and almost every home had its quilt frame ready to do duty at any time. "On my third roll" meant that the quilt had been rolled three times on the frame and the quilter was again quilting the reachable space before another roll would be taken. Five or six rolls usually completed the process, so it was easy to judge a friend's progress. When a neighbor remarked that she was "about to take out," it meant that the quilting was finished and the quilt would soon be taken out of the frame.

Quilt designs were eagerly exchanged, for even the most ambitious quiltmaker could not hope to make a quilt like all those she admired. So instead she collected the patterns, and patterns were often far from simple, just as the quilt itself had ceased to be simple. With all its far-reaching ramifications, the quilt had become a complex and subtle factor in the society of a growing land.

> The feminine love of color, the longing for decoration, as well as pride in skill of needlecraft, found riotous expression in quilt-making. Women reveled in intricate and difficult patchwork . . . they talked over the designs, admired pretty bits of calico, and pondered what combinations to make.[3]

Much rivalry ensued as quiltmakers vied to see who could have the greatest number of pieces in their quilts, which often reached into the thousands. We read of almost incredible attainments, such as quilts containing around thirty thousand pieces, each piece measuring one-fourth inch by three-fourths inch.

It was not only the women with means and leisure who indulged in this absorbing pastime. Many a woman had to "make her time" to spend on recreation, as the making of fancy quilts came to be considered. Ellen Emeline Webster, in a delightful talk on quilts, gave an account of a quilt that was made entirely on Mondays. It was made by a woman who passionately loved color and found great pleasure in

PLATE 32
Black Velvet Victorian Quilt. This most unusual patchwork and embroidered quilt is said to have been made by Miss Celestine Bacheller of Wyoma, a part of Lynn, Massachusetts, between 1850 and 1900. Miss Bacheller was born in 1840, and it is thought that she made her "pictures in stitches" of familiar houses and gardens in her neighborhood, perhaps of her own home. The designs are graphically treated, even to a miniature awning that can be lifted and sails on a sailing vessel that can be shifted. Courtesy of the Boston Museum of Fine Arts.

fashioning bright pieces to go into her quilts. To quote Miss Webster, a New Englander and a descendant of the maker of the quilt, "There was a time in New England when it was considered positively wicked to indulge in anything from which one derived pleasure for oneself. One might work to please others, but to do so for one's own sake was sinful." This woman, so the story goes, had been chided by others, perhaps including the preacher, for the time she was spending on her quilts. So she resolved to work on her quilt only on Mondays, which was the hardest day of the week, and only after the necessary chores had been done— the washing, scrubbing, cooking, and mending, and even extra chores she imposed on herself to do on that day. Then only did she feel justified in working on her treasure. The "Monday Quilt" contained between two and three thousand pieces.

The quilt was made for every conceivable reason. All the quiltmaker needed was an excuse. For example, the Friendship Quilt, the Album Quilt, the Autograph Quilt all stemmed from the same idea. Each square or block would be designed or executed by a different friend or relative, usually signed and carrying some appropriate message. In this same category were the Presentation quilts, composed of squares made by admirers of a prominent or worthy person, such as a teacher or minister. The squares were then set together, forming the quilt top, and the finished product was presented to the honored one as a testament of his followers' esteem.

Such community-minded quilts became valued and significant keepsakes and have been of help to more than one researcher proving without doubt some lost link in the family genealogy. Here, worked in fine stitches, were recorded authoritative facts.

As rivalry among the makers of different squares played a lively part, the results were often spectacular and most elaborate. This type of quiltmaking reached a phenomenal degree of perfection in the Maryland area. It was, however, popular in all parts of the country, many examples have survived, and each is an authoritative record of early Americana.

Sentiment and religion ran high throughout the vogue. A typical verse from an Album Quilt, dated 1852, reads:

> Should I be parted from thee
> Look at this and think of me
> May I twine a wreath for thee
> Sacred to love and memory.

Good advice was contained in a quilt given to Cousin Walker Washington of Carolina County, Virginia, a young man going to college. One square reads:

> Ask Heaven, Virtue, Health,
> But never let your prayer be Wealth.

And Miss Selma H. Talliferro of Westmoreland, Virginia, wrote on her square, dated June 11, 1849:

> A man too careful of danger
> Liveth in continued torment
> But a cheerful expecter of the best
> Hath a fountain of joy within him.

From Nantucket, Massachusetts, that "Little Grey Lady of the Sea," there has come down to Paul Blackmur from his whaling grandfather's family an Autograph Quilt. It is beautifully embroidered with beehives, birds, and flower baskets, tumbling with such roses as bloom only on Nantucket Island. The quilt blocks are signed by both men and women—one that speaks of the Civil War period was signed by "W. H. Wood 3rd Battalion Rifles M V M Co. A 1861–1873," while another fancy square was done by "Little Nanny Worth, aged 6 years and 6 months."

The sentiments speak unmistakably of the surrounding sea such as:

> May the bark of our friendship never founder
> on the rock of deceit.

> Let the deep waters of oblivion roll
> On all that grieves or irritates thy soul.

Another Massachusetts Autograph Quilt from the seafaring locale of Gloucester reflects the influence of the ever-present sea. The quilt serves as a historical recording of the old families who helped to make Gloucester, "preeminently queen of the fishing ports" in the nineteenth century—Ellery, Forbes, Procter, Haskell, Davis, and Friend. It is among the treasures to be found in the Capt. Elias Davis House (c. 1800), a part of the impressive Cape Ann Historical Association Museum. The verses are written to Georgiania Ellery Friend on the squares that make up her 1849 quilt:

> Christ is a strong tower
> The righteous flee into it and are safe
> May Georgiania be one of that happy number.

And,

> May thy path through life be in the sunshine
> of fortune
> May soft breezes waft thy gilded bark o'er
> a smooth sea to a guileless peaceful shore.

The Victorians with their special penchant for the

PLATE 33
Victorian Crazy Quilt. This is an unusually good example of the period, featuring silks, satins, and velvets in a "crazy" pattern with much gold interspersed and many designs of intricate stitchery, including butterflies and tennis racquets. Offen Collection.

sentimental often carried it to the point of morbidness. Memory Wreath quilts developed along with other strange customs relative to keeping alive the memory of "dear departed ones." The squares which composed the memory quilt often utilized scraps of clothing once belonging to the one "gone before." They boasted beautiful and lovingly embroidered motifs appropriate to sorrow, and were apt to carry the name and death date of the one being commemorated.

All this was in line with the prevailing fashion of decorated "mourning pictures," which so graphically depicted the grieving ones under the weeping willow tree beside the gravestone, on which were carved the names of the deceased as well as other members of the family no longer with them. In line, also, was the very expensive custom of presenting gifts of "mourning jewelry" containing locks of hair of loved ones to friends and relatives.

A somber Widow's Quilt, fashioned of sober grays, comes under this weird category. It is an American-made quilt, originally from nineteenth-century New Jersey, but is now a part of the very comprehensive collection of American quilts owned by the American Museum in Bath, England. Poignantly enough, the Widow's Quilt is very narrow, made for a single bed. The dominant appliquéd motif, the lyre signifying mourning, is accented with Death's Dark Darts done in black.

Naturally the little, narrow Widow's Quilt is one that stays in one's mind, and brings forth a sad smile at the frailty of mankind and his almost reveling in the celebration of death.

We cannot, however, be too quick to censure American Victorians for morbidness. The custom of mourning beds dressed in black hangings, black coverlets, and even sheets dates back to the seventeenth century in England. According to Marie D. Webster, "These funeral articles of furniture were quite expensive and it was a friendly custom to lend these mourning beds to families in time of affliction."[4] Mrs. Webster quotes from a letter written in 1644 from a Mrs. Eure to her nephew, Sir Ralph Verney:

> Sweet nephew, I am now overrun with miserys and troubles, but the greatest misfortune that could happen to me was the death of the gallantest man [her husband] that I ever knew.

Whereupon Sir Ralph, in great sympathy, "offers her the loan of the great black bed and hangings from Clafton."[5]

As the nineteenth century was drawing to a close and Victorianism was intensified, quiltmakers resorted to the greatest extremes in order to create something novel. There are examples of quilts made entirely from silk cigar bands. Many ladies fashioned quilts from silk neckties.

I have seen a unique quilt composed of silk shoe labels, those little printed or woven labels that were sewn inside the linings of shoes, advertising to the world the trade name as well as the name of the manufacturer. The quilt was a product of Brockton, Massachusetts, known as the "Shoe City" during the period when shoe manufacturing flourished in New England. Also in the same area of the large shoe plants were many factories solely devoted to the making of shoe findings. One of these was Tolman's Print factory which received orders from all over the world for their fine silk labels. Mrs. Joyce Tomlinson of Brockton utilized these pieces of varicolored ribbons and succeeded in creating a fascinating and unique Log Cabin quilt of two thousand labels bearing the names of stores from every state in the Union as well as many foreign countries. This unusual bit of Americana is a memento of one of America's important industries and attests to the American quiltmaker's ingenuity.

Another unusual variation of the novel is a quilt made by Miss Anne H. Chapin, an accomplished bell ringer of Kent, Connecticut. The quilt is designed as a musical composition for bell ringers to follow, the different colors designating the notes for the musical theme, and the three bands of color on the edges, red, green, and white, signifying the first colors of the bell ropes.

But it was not only women who were caught up in the quilt mania. Quilts have always appealed to men. Even today, a man's typical reaction upon being shown a quilt is apt to be a wistful remembrance as he remarks, "I remember a red and white star quilt my mother made," or "I cut quilt pieces for my grandmother when I was a boy." Once when President Dwight D. Eisenhower was visiting his birthplace in Denison, Texas, now a national museum, he ran his hand over the old quilt design called Jacob's Ladder, saying, "My brother Milton and I helped cut the scraps that went into this quilt."

Taking pride in their ladies' accomplishments, it was often the menfolk who encouraged the quiltmakers to press on to more intricate patterns and more striking colors, and they, too, became quiltmakers.

In Florence Peto's authoritative volume, *Historic Quilts*,[6] a whole chapter is devoted to "Quilts Designed

and Made by Men." These gentlemen quiltmakers include men of all types and backgrounds from Obàdiah Smith, farmer and lover of music, who made his Triple Hexagonal Star in 1788, to Captain James Darling of Smithtown, Long Island, who drew his Compass Star pattern for the quilt to be made by his daughter while he was away on a long sea voyage. Mary Jane's reward upon his return was a lovely silk dress. In the meantime she had also acquired a husband. Into the middle of her father's compass stars, she had very cleverly incorporated the heart motif, a sure sign of matrimony.

Other male quiltmakers mentioned by Mrs. Peto are the Reverend Sebastian Cabot Hanes, a minister who loved to study the heavens and developed his Wonder of the Sky pattern, and E. R. Dickinson, a retired businessman who made at least seven quilts. However, it would seem that the peak of the mania had been reached in the accomplishment in 1839 of Albert Small of Ottawa, Illinois, whose Mosaic composition contained 63,460 patches, each the size of ten-cent pieces before the seams were taken.

The late Dr. William Rush Dunton, Jr., another gentleman enamored of quilts, was a well-known psychiatrist, whose interest in the art began when he found that quiltmaking was of real therapeutic value in the treatment of his patients. In his book, *Old Quilts*, he tells of Charles Pratt of Philadelphia, who made thirty-three Biblical picture quilts, each reaching the almost incredible number of thirty thousand pieces.[7]

We cannot allow ladies to be outdone by the men—least of all in the matter of quiltmaking. So, it would seem that the gentlemen's record had been outstripped by Mrs. Grace McConce Snyder of North Platte, Nebraska. Mrs. Snyder, a lady of ninety years, is a maker of fabulous quilts. Her finest example, a Petit Point quilt of eighty-seven thousand pieces, is nothing short of a Wonder of the World and has most deservedly taken many national prizes.

In such an atmosphere of over-decoration and novel effects, it is no wonder that the crazy quilt should have developed and rampaged across the country to such an extent that even the period could be termed the crazy-quilt era. Not that the crazy quilt was something new. Far from it. It was the common ancestor of the quilt in America, born of necessity. But during the last quarter of the nineteenth century and during the dawning years of the twentieth, the crazy quilt became something quite different. There was nothing lowly or common about it now. Achieving the epitome of elegance, it had been promoted to the parlor. Called by various fancy names, it was a slumber robe, a couch throw, a creation to be displayed—an important accessory in the latest heterogeneous scheme of decorating.

It must hold its own amid sumptuous interiors crowded to overflowing with whatnots and knick-knacks; it must be worthy of the beaded portieres, the mammoth gilt-framed pictures and the draped mantelpieces with their collections of gewgaws. Women had attained leisure, the crazy quilt was their favorite pastime, and quiltmaking had reached the zenith of its popularity. The aim was to see who could lavish the greatest amount of hand-painted adornment and intricate stitchery upon her silk and velvet masterpieces. Lessons in hand painting were popular. Publications devoted to "Fancy Designs" and "Ornamental

Oriental Work"[8] guided the ladies in the execution of the Kensington stitch; the catch-all; French knots; featherstitching, single, double and triple; the herring bone; buttonhole; catstitch; loops and diamonds. Friends exchanged unusual stitches along with the swapping of choice scraps of materials.

During the craze, great numbers of fine examples were made. Almost every family has inherited at least one significant piece, and many are cherished today by descendants of the makers for the loving stitchery lavished upon them.

It was not only in the world of quilting and decorating, however, that drastic reversals had taken place. Even in architecture the changing times were leaving their indelible imprint in the form of Mansard-roofed buildings and Victorian mansions boasting meaningless cupolas and turrets, much gingerbread and jigsawed fretwork.

Household furnishings were designed, for better or for worse, often worse, with a determination to be different. It was the era when the beautiful colonial pieces of classic design were discarded or sent to the attic and the ambition of householders was to acquire new, machine-made, golden-oak furniture and mission sets, as well as the new, shining brass beds.

In a time of unbridled innovation, it was only natural that the early handmade quilts should come to be looked upon as common and relegated to the attic or used with such little care that they were soon worn out. The up-to-the-minute housewife even preferred the new Marseilles all-white bedspreads coming from the Jacquard looms, and if she could not afford such a store-bought spread to put on the metal bed that had

supplanted the old four-poster, she was apt to use a quilt, carrying its pattern in color on the wrong or white side, pattern down, in imitation of these machine-woven counterpanes. Customs were rapidly changing and by the time the twentieth century was in full swing, it was no longer fashionable to devote oneself to the producing of quilts, crazy or otherwise. Whatever the cause or causes (and there were many), this was true for the first time in the history of America.

Women who had been forced to become involved in a World War that broke down all barriers, socially, physically, and geographically had by the twenties transferred their energies to more active pursuits. And, by the forties, the quilt had fallen into such disrepute or anonymity that comparatively few people could recall "the glory that was the quilt." It was only a faded memory or an amusing bit of Americana. Even for utilitarian purposes no one was really interested and for the most part the ladies had come to prefer store-bought "comforters" for practicality. Even in the mountains of Appalachia, a stronghold where the making of quilts had once been an exciting and vital part of life, it was hard to find women who were even conversant with the old arts of patchwork and quilting.

Just as reverses of fortune can come to the best and most prosperous of families, so they came to quilting in the first half of the twentieth century. It was to be many years before patchwork and the patchwork quilt would be able to recover their rightful place in the folk art of America.

VII
Renaissance

We have traced the evolution of the quilt in America from its earliest beginnings when it served the dual purposes of providing warmth and satisfying an innate longing for beauty. We have seen quiltmaking pass through various important social stages, reflecting the historical events the quiltmakers themselves were experiencing. We have watched it become a vital and all-absorbing activity until it reached a point of mania. Perhaps its very popularity was conducive to its near demise—it became too much of a good thing.

But during the almost complete erasure of the quilt from its dominant role, its potential did not die. There were those who still cared, faithful followers of the art who never allowed it to die—individuals who continued to indulge in making quilts. One needed only to visit a national, regional, state, or county fair to see fine examples of quilts on exhibit, some old and some new, and the crowds coming to view them belied the seeming indifference on the part of so many Americans.

During the years, there would appear occasional stories in both national and local publications—accounts of groups that gathered together, either through a church or for purely social reasons, for the sheer pleasure of working on quilts. Groups scattered in communities throughout the country—stretching from the hills of the Ozarks to historic Lexington, Massachusetts, George's Mill in New Hampshire to Glen Alice, Tennessee; White Hall, Illinois, to Mount Joy, Pennsylvania; Glasco, Kansas, to Horse Cave, Kentucky—giving indication that this very human document was surviving to a certain degree.

There were various other ways in which interest in the quilt was preserved. Many old quilts were saved from extinction through the diligence and foresight of quilt lovers who made a point of collecting them. Old handmade quilts were often used in the most menial and profligate ways—as ironing-board covers, padding for wagon seats to ease rides over jolting roads, packing and covering furniture, especially when moving.

Jonathan Holstein and Gail van der Hoof, who have become internationally known for their collection of hundreds of pieced quilts representative of abstract art forms and whose exhibit at the Whitney Museum attracted worldwide attention, gathered many of their items from the most obscure places. "They stalk them in junk and antique shops, flush them in flea markets, pick them from off barn floors and from the backs of trucks when they sometimes spot them swathing furniture."[1]

One avid collector in the state of Maryland, an area

"noted the world over as a happy hunting ground for fine quilt specimens,"[2] was Dr. Dunton of whom I have spoken before. Over a period of time, he sought out old and rare examples, collecting and photographing more than five hundred, especially the Album quilts that reached such a high state of perfection in Maryland in the mid–1800's. Included among Dr. Dunton's finds was the pride of a sea captain, a quilt that had made the trip around Cape Horn three times.

Miss Bertha Amelia Meckstroth of Chicago was a devotee of quilts. Her unique collection of eighty-nine quilts was given equally to Barat College in Lake Forest, Illinois, and to Radcliffe College in Cambridge, Massachusetts. Through the sale of these quilts after her death, many people have been given the pleasure of seeing them, and the funds from the sale, which were considerable, have been used for scholarships.

And what of the quilt today?

One can hardly pick up a current publication without being aware of the amazing revival of interest in patchwork quilts and patchwork in general, resulting in an apparently boundless resurgence of activity. And perhaps no form of the home decorative arts can offer greater opportunity for creative expression than the patchwork quilt—in color, design, or the artistic whole. Both women and men are organizing in groups, or as individuals going it alone, commercially or for purely personal pleasure—recreating the old patchwork patterns or creating new ones expressive of today's world. No doubt it is a part of the revolt against stereotyped, impersonal, factory-made things, and in a do-it-yourself world it threatens to reach a state of craze rivaling that of the crazy-quilt era. The great hope is that the revival sweeping the country in this, as well as the burgeoning interest being shown in all the handicrafts, may stem from an honest base of artistic understanding along with the growing desire for something better and more significant.

In an article by Rita Reif in *The New York Times* one basic reason is given for its popularity:

> Patchwork quilting, a symbol of thrift to American women since Pilgrim days, has, in revival, come to mean economic liberation—and other things—to hundreds, perhaps thousands. The majority of the women benefiting from the continuing interest are among the nation's poorest. For them—blacks in Alabama, whites in Appalachia and most recently the Wahpeton–Sioux Indians in South Dakota— quilting cooperatives and nonprofit organizations offer a route out of poverty.[3]

There are dividends from the widespread revival that cannot be measured from the economic point of view. Just as quiltmaking in colonial times came to be a community activity with the quilting bees establishing bonds of friendship, so today they become the most important means of friendly contacts in both townships and countryside. Handcrafts by Tract, at Webster, South Dakota, is a group of eight hundred sewing women (five hundred part-time and three hundred full-time workers—of which about one-third are Indians) whose coordinator, S. Robert Pearson, declares, "There is a renewed sense of community here. For the first time, white women and Indian women are sitting down together and working side by side . . . learning to respect and understand each other."[4]

On the Oglala Indian Reservation at Pine Ridge, South Dakota, the ladies of the Red Cloud–Wakpami

Quilting Association are also busy making copies of the traditional quilt patterns. In 1971, on the cover of an issue of *The Journal of the American Medical Association*,[5] pictured in color was the old design, Drunkard's Trail (or Wanderer's Path), a quilt made by Mrs. Shirley Piper and Mrs. Ella He Crow.

Headquarters for the all-black cooperative, Martin Luther King Freedom Quilting Bee,[6] are in Alberta, Alabama, where twenty-five members spend up to seven hours a day producing quilts that are merchandised through stores in the East, their sales in a year amounting to twenty-nine thousand dollars.

While the natural habitat for the quilt is Appalachia, the realm of quiltmaking today is not confined to the East, or to the Appalachian range. Western mountains and windswept prairies are producing coverlets that speak of their own land: Rocky Mountain Road, Western Sunburst, Prairie Patch. A group of workers in Whitehall, Illinois, have chosen the picturesque name of Storm[7] and are truly sewing up a storm of enthusiam with effective results.

In California, Judy Raffael, a stained-glass artist who has become enamoured of the quilt, invited seventy women to come together for a sew-in to collaborate on quilts, with the result that their finished products are on exhibit, touring the country, and the caption of a magazine article telling of their activity reads, "Many Hands Make Bright Works for Artists and Friends."

It is not a different story today, only updated. Women are pleased and proud to be earning good money, having careers at home while engaged in a needlecraft that has been inherently theirs ever since

PLATE 35
Octagons or Hour Glasses. A striking quilt, c. 1870, composed of brilliant red and white octagons and triangles, made by Clara Rivest while she attended school in L'Assomption, Province of Quebec. Such starkly designed old quilts seem as new as today's most modern tastes. Their rediscovery has contributed much to the patchwork renaissance. This example is also beautifully quilted with floral designs and the maker's monogram in some of the octagonal pieces. It was inherited by Mrs. Theodore R. Lockwood of Newton, Massachusetts, a niece of the maker. Bacon Collection.

the early settlers claimed the mountains for their homeland, and the women set to work contriving enough "kivvers" to keep warm. Their enthusiasm runs high while their piecin' and patchin' keep up with the times. Quilt names are undergoing change as they always have, to meet changing conditions. Grandmother's quilt might have been a Flying Kite but now it's more apt to be Airplane or Up and Away.

The boast and the belief of the Women of Community Aid on Lookout Mountain, Tennessee, is "The Art of Quilting is an Old Appalachian Custom."[8] Furthermore, "Our colors are prettier and our stitches smaller and we do 'trapunto.'" It is their sincere aim to keep up the high standards set by their quilting grandmothers and not allow the art to deteriorate. For they think of it as an art instead of a business, expressing it this way: "There is so much labor involved in making a quilt, you've got to love it to be good." These aims have paid off well, and the women can rightfully take pride in the results when they are told by the elite decorators and fashionable shops that handle their work, "Don't show your things elsewhere. We can keep you busy."

At holiday seasons, the orders come in such volume that the ladies from the Lookout Mountain Baptist Church join the group to help. Stopping only long enough for a hot lunch, Mrs. Mitchell Simmons says, "Those lunches together on the days of quilting and talking make you know why the old-fashioned quilting bees were so much fun."

There are many groups in many sections of Appalachia, but one of the most effective organizations is in West Virginia, the Mountain Artisans, involving some two hundred women and covering an area of seven counties. The enthusiastic support of Mrs. John D. Rockefeller IV gives impetus to the whole project.

It was a hot day in midsummer when I visited the business headquarters in downtown Charleston, the capital of the state. Occupying one floor of a large building, it hummed with activity. Here the designing and the cutting are done, and about twenty workers (mostly young) were darting in and out and around huge cutting tables among ceiling-high stacks of bolts of fascinating materials and accessories.

Once the patterns are drawn and cut, the work is carried out by fieldworkers to the fifteen different sewing groups which are scattered in communities and bear down-to-earth names peculiar to the mountains: Sod Sewing Ladies, Dogbone Sewing Group, Big Creek Sewing Co-op, Willing Workers of Pipestem, Women of Wyoming at Mullins, Village Stitchery, Sew and Sew Ladies of Upshur County.

All the activity has been greatly publicized. One national publication entitled it, "West Virginia Super-Sewing Bee,"[9] while another spoke of it poetically as "A Bloom in Appalachia."[10] The news media have heralded it as an "Anti-Poverty Success."[11] It has also been called "A Dream Come True."[12] Between these last two lies the truth that gives the project such deep appeal. Certainly it is no welfare program, but it has helped many a woman to get off welfare rolls. One worker said, "It's brought back pride to the mountains."

As with many groups, Mountain Artisans are reaching out beyond quilts, although quilts are still their most important product (some priced in four figures) (Plate 37). The clothes defy description. Appliquéd dresses are composed of combinations of materials that, at first glance, seem utterly foreign to one another—velvet, cotton, ribbon, and leather, resulting in a look reminiscent of elaborate garments of medieval times when patchwork, appliqué, quilting, and embroidery were all joined to create a lavish richness.

All over the country professional designers are making use of old quilt designs for every conceivable commodity. Patchwork adorns not only women's clothing but men's fashionable trousers. The son of the family has a patchwork hunting shirt and jeans, while the daughter has patched denims as well as a very feminine pieced evening frock. Exclusive gift shops feature patchwork pillows in every style and size, including enormous floor pillows, and stuffed animals, bikinis, tablecloths, and handbags.

Quilt designs are the inspiration for all sorts of commercially produced articles—writing paper, wrapping papers, place mats, playing cards—just name it. Truly distinctive is a recent wallpaper design by Philip Graf of New York. He has most successfully done a hand-printed paper called Quilting Bee, impervious to water and stains. The design was executed by Scott Nutter of Connecticut, inspired by Nutter's grandmother's crazy quilt. Every charming detail has been retained—autographs of fond aunts and other relatives and all the fancy stitchery.

Patchwork has become an investment—big business! But also, once again, it is an accepted folk art, perhaps America's most indigenous and vital one, enthusiastically received north, south, east, and west.

What should be of the most lasting importance, more than the social and commercial acceptance of the patchwork quilt or the monetary value now being placed upon it, is the new awareness of its "significant contribution to American artistic achievement" in the

PLATE 36

Block Pattern. Composed of brilliant silks, this unfinished quilt top is an exuberant Victorian version of Baby's Blocks in an unfinished quilt top owned by Herbert Offen, whose interests include both quilt collecting and horse breeding. He said when he showed it to me that he intended to use it for his racing silks when his newest colt, "Hasty Success," made her debut. Offen Collection.

world of abstract art. Museums in all parts of the country are now proud to exhibit examples and to be a part of the great revival—from the Greenville County Museum in South Carolina,[13] to the magnificent Shelbourne Museum in Vermont; the Baltimore Museum in Maryland[14] to the Whitney Museum of American Art in New York City.[15]

At the time of the exhibit at the Whitney in the summer of 1971, the art critics were startled to recognize its significance. Hilton Kramer wrote in *The New York Times*:

> What is so impressive is not the originality of the design . . . but the dazzling sensibility for color and visual construction that the execution of these designs, with their personal and regional variations, display with such appealing vigor. For a century or more preceding the self-conscious invention of pictorial abstraction in European painting the anonymous quiltmakers of the American provinces created a remarkable succession of visual masterpieces that anticipated many forms that were later prized for their originality and courage.
>
> The exhibition is not only full of unusual visual pleasures but is the kind of exhibition that prompts us to rethink the relation of high art to what are customarily regarded as lesser forms of visual expression. This is an issue that any historian of American art is going to have to come to terms with in future dealings with his subject and one is grateful to the Whitney for pressing the issue upon us.
>
> Among the quilts the esthetic quality is generally so high that it would be foolishly arbitrary to single out particular examples. For connoisseurs, the show will confirm what they already know—that this is one medium in which American folk imagination excelled. For newcomers the show will be a stunning revelation.[16]

PLATE 37

Jamie Rockefeller's Animal Quilt. This brilliant quilt features flowers as well as animals in a composition of twenty squares done in a combination of appliqué, embroidery, and quilting. Made by the Mountain Artisans of West Virginia at the request of Sharon Percy Rockefeller for the Rockefellers' first-born, it was designed by Dorothy Weatherford. The work was started in early summer 1969, Jamie was born in July, 1969, and it took over a year to finish the quilt. Made for a child's bed, it presently serves as a wall hanging in the Rockefeller home. From The Mountain Artisans Quilting Book by Alfred Allan Lewis, published by the Macmillan Company, 1973.

Now the interest has spread abroad. The same exhibit of pieced quilts which received acclaim in New York at the Whitney was shown at the Louvre in Paris the following summer. It was a spectacular success. The quilt was no longer in the category of a craft. It is a recognized art form.

VIII
Making Quilts

Quilt (deriving from the Latin *culcita*), counterpane, coverlid, coverlet (from the French *couvre lit*) are used interchangeably throughout this book. However, the words are often understood to have different meanings.

A coverlet (although it may be quilted) is thought of as an unquilted bedspread, some collectors defining it as made of any woven material, generally wool. From coverlet, especially one with a lining kept in place by stitches passing through both layers, there derived the words quilt and counterpane, stemming from medieval quiltpoint or counterpoint.

Coverlid in folk etymology is a bedspread.

But for our purposes, we give Webster's definition: "A quilt is a bed coverlet made of two layers of cloth of which the top one is usually pieced or appliquéd and having a filling of wool, cotton, or down held in place by stitched designs or tufts worked through all thicknesses."

For people who have some basic knowledge of quilt-making, these facts may be sufficient, but for others some explanation may be helpful. Many times after speaking on the subject of quilts I have been surprised to find how little is known about their actual making. The question is asked, plaintively, "But how do I go about *making* one?"

First, it must be made clear that there are two distinct operations to construct a quilt, and they are two very separate arts. One is the composing of the quilt top, or patchwork, and the other is the quilting of it.

Almost in the same breath, a second question follows the first, "Shall I make a 'pieced' quilt or a 'patched,' and what is the difference?"

This is a natural query for, as has been said before, there are also two distinct methods of making patchwork, quite dissimilar in effect when finished.

PIECED QUILTS

A simple definition of a pieced quilt is that it is one made by sewing pieces or patches together, using a running stitch on the wrong side, in all probability the oldest type used in America. The piecing can be done either in a haphazard fashion regardless of color and cloth, or in a crazy fashion however the pieces happen to fit.

Perhaps these two types are the easiest of all quilts to make, and with the current interest in patchwork "bustin' out all over," they are very much in vogue today, as in the days of our original American patchwork. In all likelihood, the majority of early utilitarian

PLATE 38
Hexagonal Mosaic. Although its ancestry reaches back to England, this pattern has become universally loved all over America and is commonly known as Grandmother's Flower Garden. An excellent version in the Metropolitan Museum in New York is called Mosaic, while other names are French Bouquet and Honey Comb. The two details of this carefully wrought example, unfinished, show the technique of paperbacking. The first step is the shaping of each hexagonal piece over the paper. They are then joined with whipping stitch to form a larger motif. In silk quilts, the paper is often left in the quilt top. In cotton quilts, if paper is used, it is removed when the quilt top is finished.
Bacon Collection.

quilts were made in these styles, often of woolen pieces, using the unworn parts of worn-out garments to obtain warmth so that every precious scrap of cloth might be saved.

If the choice is a pieced quilt, and the maker wishes to carry out a design, whether in wool, cotton, or silk, greater artistic effort and skill and usually more fabric are required than in a crazy quilt. Simple basic designs—the square, rectangle, triangle, diamond—are often used for practical quiltmaking but may be arranged to form complicated and elaborate designs.

For instance, a four-patch, upon which so many little girls learned to sew (formed of four squares set together), can be the basis for extremely attractive quilts. A nine-patch (nine squares set together) demands that four intersections meet.

Secondary designs include the circle, hexagon, octagon, and others, and require considerable skill in piecing—"getting them to fit together pretty," as one quiltmaker expressed it.

The quiltmakers of past generations showed much imagination as well as ability in their designing of their pieced quilts, many of which resemble the abstract art forms so popular in our modern world.[1] While some received inspiration from their gardens or nature, others of a mathematical turn of mind enjoyed working out the geometrical patterns, perhaps with the help of their menfolk.

APPLIQUÉD QUILTS

The second type of patchwork quilt is not so easy to define. The patched or appliquéd quilt is also re-

PLATE 39
Hexagonal Mosaic. The reverse side of the design on Plate 38, showing the paper backing cut from newspapers, labels, and letters, and basting stitches as well as the tiny whipping stitches. Bacon Collection.

ferred to as sewed on, or laid on, or applied work. As its name implies, it is made by cutting the design to be used from one fabric and applying it (or patching it) on another—often patch upon patch. The applying is usually done with an invisible whipping stitch, although the patch design may be applied with a buttonhole stitch, cording, or other fancy stitchery.[2]

In America, the appliquéd quilt came into great favor around the middle of the eighteenth century, reaching its height in the 1850's and 1860's, just before the Civil War. It was especially favored in the South and is usually conceded to be the aristocrat of quiltdom. It has been said, "A woman's pieced quilts were her everyday interest, but her patched (appliquéd) her glory." Certainly the appliqué type requires more cloth and new cloth rather than leftovers, to cut and apply the appliqué patterns—a process that has led some husbands to exclaim, "What in the world is the use of cutting up new cloth and sewing it back together again?"

Both pieced and appliquéd come under the art of patchwork, and sometimes the two methods are combined. There are interesting and handsome examples of both and it is not easy to answer, "Which shall I make, a pieced or a patched?" The freedom of the appliquéd, which allows for beauty and grace of line in patterns—birds, flowers, and scrolls—appeals to some, and the applying of several layers of materials gives a rich look, reminiscent of the impressive patchwork of medieval times.

Others are attracted to the pieced, which conforms to a definite pattern, and many feel that the pieced variety is more expressive of our American history.

PLATE 40
Opposite: *Unfinished Victorian Crazy Quilt. Used here was a technique often employed, that of lining each piece with a thin fabric backing to serve as a foundation before the pieces are set together. This gives the whole quilt body while in the making and strength after it is completed. This quilt, finished, would have the points of the diamond shapes along the edge, adding a special fillip to the whole effect.* Offen Collection.

PLATE 41
Overleaf: *Texas Lone Star. Fashioned of sateen, in Yellow Rose of Texas colors, this was made in Silverton, Texas, in 1922, for Lula Jeannette Julian, a gift from her aunt, Jennie Lee Peek Fisher. Maker and quilter are unknown.* Courtesy of Jeannette Moskow.

There are as many reasons and considerations in choosing a quilt design as there are individuals. And today, there are individuals who are creating their own, expressive of their personalities.

This is what one ambitious young woman, Mrs. Alice Usher of Indianapolis, Indiana, has done. Moreover, she has made a pair for twin beds. After studying many of the old conventional designs, she felt that none held significance for her so she determined to design her own. She was especially fond of the beautiful flower, freesia, and developed a stunning stylized freesia. She had always admired the old Turkey red and white quilts, so she developed her freesia in red and appliquéd it on a white background. The result is a striking quilt, equally attractive with modern or antique furnishings.

Another modern quiltmaker chose a pattern that had been used for several generations in her family, a charming original version of the Little Red Schoolhouse, designed by the great-great uncle of the little boy whose proud possession it now is.

The dainty Dresden Plate is a combination of both types of patchwork. The plate, pieced together, is applied on the white background of the square. The pattern appealed to a young mother for her daughter's quilt and certainly it will be a cherished treasure, including the colorful pieces from her little-girl cotton frocks.

Choosing materials for the quilt top should be done with care, bearing in mind two things: first, a firm weave that will not ravel easily, and second, a texture that is not too closely woven or too heavy to quilt. These precautions will help in cutting small triangles

PLATE 42
Previous page: *Kentucky Flowerpot. A quilt created by Rebecca Kenrick Tarwater of Rockwood, Tennessee, during her revival of quiltmaking in the first quarter of the twentieth century. On Plate 44, another quilt of the same design shows how differently the same pattern may be executed by two different makers. This is one of the fascinating features of quilts—there are never two alike.* Bacon Collection.

PLATE 43
Opposite: *Basket Quilt. The basket design has always been a favorite with quiltmakers. This is an example, c. 1840, of unusually fine work, done in earth-color patches. Noteworthy also are the arrangement of the designs and the border.* Laurenzi Collection.

Making Quilts

or diamonds where a part of each must be on the bias. It is not easy to fit bias sides of sleazy rayon, thin voile, or crepe into squares or to attempt with such material to turn the edges of an intricate floral design for an appliquéd quilt. Using a template cut from fine-grained sandpaper to avoid slippage in cutting the designs can be helpful.

For convenience in handling, nearly every quilt top, whether pieced or patched (appliquéd), is composed of a number of blocks or squares of regular size and form.[3] Each of these units may have a design complete in itself or be only a part of a large and complicated pattern covering the whole. Very often an appropriate border, like a picture frame, around the quilt is added.

After the blocks are finished they are joined to make the body of the quilt—the quilt top.

QUILTING

The next step (the second operation) is the quilting, which rivals in importance the making of the quilt top. Quilting is the joining of the quilt top, the lining, and the interlining by the running of stitches through the three layers of materials.[4]

In America the customary and effective method of quilting was, and still is, to place the three thicknesses in a rectangular quilting frame large enough to stretch the entire coverlet. It consists of four wooden bars (made of hardwood with a smooth finish). A small hole about one-half inch in diameter in the end of each bar is helpful so that when the bars are assembled they can be held in place with four wooden pegs.

PLATE 44
Kentucky Flowerpot. Made for Robert Elisha Acuff, born in 1930 in Kentucky. Although the quilt is not antique, the old-fashioned colors (red, orange, pink, and green) of the design combine to give it an unusually quaint and charming look. (See also Plate 42.)
Courtesy of Reece Ingram Acuff.

However, I have seen quilters use the simpler method of tying the bars into position. The corners of the bars overlap, and the two longer bars are covered with heavy material such as ticking, to which the lining of the quilt is basted securely so there will be no sagging. As the work progresses, the frame must be readjusted, and these bars are rolled.

The construction of quilting frames varied, of course. Sometimes the frame was suspended from the ceiling so that it could be lifted out of the way when not in use. If, however, the homemaker had an extra room where the frame could be set up and not disturbed, the four corners of the frame might rest on the backs of chairs (often ladder-back type) of the proper height, or on wooden horses constructed for the purpose, while some frames were made with stationary legs.

Today with changing conditions, quilt frames, too, are undergoing change. Modern lap-size frames have evolved to accommodate dwellers in small quarters or apartment houses. Large embroidery hoops may serve the same purpose, allowing the quilter to quilt a portion at a time before joining all together. At the other extreme, with the popularity of king-size beds, up-to-the-minute quilters are demanding larger quilting frames.

Once the lining is stretched and basted into place in the frame, the second layer—the interlining—is laid over the lining and patted into place. This may consist of wool, cotton batting (cotton wadding), or the more modern Dacron polyester which has become extremely popular.

Cotton batting has been the usual filling for cotton

quilts in America, and it had certain advantages. It could be kept as thick as desired to give a puffed effect, or it could be pulled as thinly as needed for intricate, close stitching such as the darning stitch. The technique is a little different if Dacron is used. It requires no pulling and stays in place. A word of caution might be of help here. Do not allow the Dacron to overlap. To prevent any gaping between strips, the edges should be joined with an overcast stitch.

The third layer—the quilt top—is laid over the lining and the interlining. It is then stretched carefully so its edges can be basted firmly and evenly to the quilt lining, which has already been attached to the sidebars of the frame.

It is an exciting moment when the maker can see her quilt as a whole before she launches upon the business of quilting. In all probability, she will have been giving considerable thought to a quilting pattern that will complement her work. Even if there is to be a quilting bee, she will surely want to have something to say about the quilting pattern. For, after the completion of any quilt top there is an intermediary step. If the quilting is to be a simple running stitch, little or no planning is required. But if it is to be an elaborate quilt, calling for a complicated design (or if the quiltmaker is inexperienced even in elementary quilting), she would profit by tracing the quilting pattern lightly with a soft lead pencil (which rubs off easily) on the quilt top to guide her stitches.

If it is to be a practical, everyday type of coverlet, she may simply trace single lines (horizontally or diagonally) across the quilt, then crisscross them to form squares or diamonds. If she is an accomplished quilter however, she may pride herself on being able to run her lines freehand without tracing.

Our grandmothers learned to be ingenious in time-saving methods. To "flip a cord" meant to mark off a quilting pattern, formed of lines, by first dipping a cord in starch, drawing it tightly across the quilt top, and with a deft flip of the cord leaving an imprint of the line for the quilter to help her in forming squares and diamonds.

The evolution of quilting designs, of course, can be traced only in imagination. To obtain warmth must surely have been the original purpose of stitching three thicknesses of materials together. But the monotony of straight lines, even to form squares and diamonds, would no doubt pall on the imaginative needlewoman, and in time she developed designs which expressed her moods and her personality—some as fanciful as those she had used in designing her quilt tops. Even women of limited leisure managed to create works of real artistic merit and for those who had much time on their hands, it became a fascinating pursuit and a complicated art in itself.

It was natural that she should draw inspiration from familiar surroundings. An intriguing story of how the Ocean Wave pattern originated (and there are other versions) comes from a seaside village. A fisherman was compelled to be away for many weeks at a time, leaving his wife with her mind and eyes continually concentrated on the ocean, with the result that she introduced the obvious and graceful wave rhythm in her quilting.

Superstition, as well as sentiment, played its inevitable part in the evolvement of quilting designs just as it had with the patterns for the quilt tops. If a cable, a twisted chain, or garland of foliage were used, it was desirable that it not be broken. Such a break might foretell a life cut short by disaster.

But the cable stitch, broken or otherwise, after 1866, became so popular as a quilting design that young ladies were willing to take the risk. Cyrus Field had become the current hero. At last he had succeeded in the significant feat—the laying of the trans-Atlantic cable. No longer was he laughed at for his "wild ideas."

If the running stitches of the quilting design harmonize in line and detail with the quilt design, the beauty of the finished product is enhanced. By outlining it, the whole design is brought into greater relief. This method of quilting is especially popular today.

James E. Ayres writes in *American Coverlets* of that exacting period when extreme stress was placed on the exquisiteness of the quilting.

> Elaborate quilting designs were drawn with the help of templates made of sized paper or fabric; examples of patterns are: princess feather, star and crown, peacock fan, oak leaf, daisy, swirl, acanthus, day lily, starfish, teacup (made by overlapping circles), running vine, pineapple, spider web.[6]

I well remember a personal experience when it became necessary to learn firsthand about templates. I had just completed the top for one of the two quilts I ever attempted. My squares were all finished, my top set together, and I felt great satisfaction. I was visiting at my former home in Tennessee and all I had to do (or so I thought) was to place it in the magic hands of Mrs. Amanda Taylor, who had consented to do the quilting. I had not counted on having to cope with that intermediary step of tracing the quilting design.

The main theme consisted of four very large circles with plumed edges. In the spaces between the large designs, there would be much fine quilting, called "darning," added by Mrs. Taylor who could do this freehand.

I was totally ignorant of how to go about getting those lovely plumed-edged circles transferred to my quilt top. It was Cousin Melissa Ervin who came to my rescue and together we did it!

There was quite a trick to it, and it proved to be more easily accomplished than one might suppose from looking at the finished intricate-appearing design. Using a soft lead pencil attached to a string, we lightly drew our large circles. Then Cousin Melissa, having cut a small cardboard pattern, shell or loop-like in shape, showed me how to lay this little template around the circles, tracing loop after loop. By doing this on both sides of the circle (outside and inside) the plumed edge was achieved.

Quilting is usually done with cotton thread ranging from number fifty to number seventy, depending upon the fineness of the stitches the quilter is able to achieve. In the old days the price of the work was determined by the number of spools used, so much per spool of one hundred yards each.

The quilter sits at the edge of the frame at a height which gives her comfortable freedom to reach forward and cover the space in front of her. As the quilting proceeds, the horizontal bars are readjusted and

PLATE 45
Rose in Bud. Acquired in New England, this quilt marks a high point in the art of quiltmaking. The date is probably 1860. The subtle use of trapunto, the color, design, and technique all combine to make it most remarkable in its effect. Laurenzi Collection.

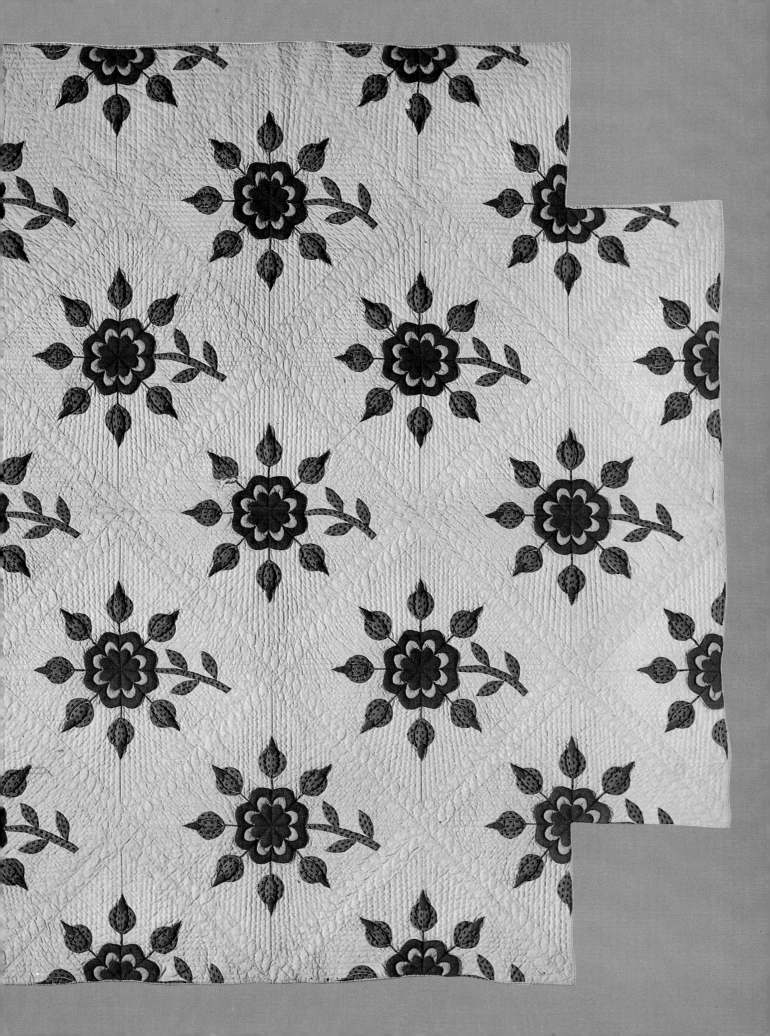

rolled so the quilter can continue to quilt the reach-able space.

As with a majority of American quilters, Mrs. Taylor quilted away from her in a running stitch as opposed to the back stitch popular in England. She used her right hand to ply the needle while holding the left hand under her work. It was by the pricking of the fingers of the left hand which acted as a guide that she could determinte and control the stitches. In the case of Mrs. Taylor, her fingers were badly pricked, but one did not need to feel sorry for her. She was extremely proud of her accomplishment.

In the history of quilting and in different locales and in different periods, various forms of quilting have been employed, including flat, corded, stuffed (trapunto), and wadding. Wadded quilting (so called because of the common use of wadded cotton for interlining) was the generally accepted type in America, but it well may be that it is being superseded by the use of modern synthetic materials. Some of the advantages and disadvantages have been referred to in this chapter and in the chapter on caring for quilts.

When the entire surface of the quilt top has been quilted, the quilt is ready to be removed from the frames. The final step is the binding of the edges, usually done with bias strips of cloth, either in white or a color that accents the colors in the design. Now, the quilt is completed.

PLAIN QUILTS

There is a third type of quilt, differing from the pieced or the patched so that it does not come under

PLATE 46
Rolling Pin and Star. Typical example of Pennsylvania-Dutch quilts, featuring hex patterns once painted on the great barns to ward away evil spirits. Made around 1870 in York, Pennsylvania. Of interest is the one purposely imperfect unit in the quilt. It was believed that only God could create a perfect thing and that anything perfect, not made by God, would be the devil's mockery. Offen Collection.

the art of patchwork, but it must be accorded a place in any attempt to tell the story of quilts. Depending entirely upon the quilting for its decorative design, the results are so distinctive that it has sometimes been called "the acme of the quilter's art." This is the plain quilt and when done in all-white it is simply called a white quilt. The quilt top is of plain cloth (as opposed to pieced or patched). Its background is European, having reached perhaps its highest development in England in the seventeenth and eighteenth centuries. Many examples, composed of colored materials, flowered or otherwise, such as silks, toiles, and polished cloth including the chintzes, are prized in museums abroad. A handsome example of a plain quilt from Salem, Massachusetts, is saffron satin (Plate 15).

The white quilt (plain quilt done in all-white cotton or linen) is the most effective in showing intricate stitchery. It came into great favor in America in the latter part of the eighteenth century and the beginning of the nineteenth.[8] Since the real beauty of the white quilt lies in the unbelievable labyrinth of stitching, padding or trapunto was used lavishly to bring into high relief certain parts of the design. (Color Plate No. 14 shows remarkably fine trapunto.) Perhaps "fine lace" is not an exaggerated description to use in attempting to convey the intricacy that was achieved in white quilts. They were done, generally speaking, by women of leisure and have been spoken of as an "art of the higher social class." But there is some evidence that women in the more humble stations of life had a share in creating them, too. In the mountainous areas of Appalachia, relief work is well known and called by the expressive term, "riz and padded."

Fortunately, outstanding examples of white quilts have survived, some privately owned and some displayed in our museums. In my opinion, the most remarkable example in America is in the Smithsonian Institution in Washington, a most appropriate place for such a treasure, and I believe all who have seen it agree. The work defies description. At least two authors, Elizabeth Calvert Hall and the previously quoted Dr. Dunton, have included it in their writings.

Miss Virginia Mason Ivy of Logan County, Kentucky, was the maker. The quilt depicts a quilted legend as stated in minute stitches on the quilt itself: "A Representation of the Fair Ground Near Russelville, Kentucky, 1856."

It was my good fortune to have known Miss Ida B. Lewis, the descendant of Miss Ivy who fell heir to this amazing quilt, and I had the privilege of studying it in detail. The body of the quilt represents the Fair Grounds, showing the gateway entrances, the judging stand, horses with riders, horses hitched to buggies, all kinds of animals, the people going to the Fair—a scene woven together with the added grace of trees and foliage—a delightful and graphic presentation of Americana. The delicacy and accuracy of detail, combined with superb workmanship, distinguish Miss Ivy as an artist of great skill. As Miss Lewis showed the quilt, she remarked, "My aunt never had art lessons. She simply loved the beautiful."

The quilt measures 7 feet 8 inches long by 7 feet 3 inches wide, and there are approximately 150 stitches in every square inch. It has been calculated

Making Quilts

by authorities who have viewed the quilt that there are 1,214,352 stitches in the whole display.

Not long before she died, Miss Lewis recounted the story of the trip by train from Massachusetts where she was then living. Accompanied by her sister, Mrs. Carrie Bretnay (both at an advanced age), she carried the quilt to Washington to deliver in person her gift to the Smithsonian.

The probable tangible reason for the decline of the white quilt was the invention of the Jacquard loom, a revolutionary development in the world of weaving. Invented and perfected by Joseph Marie Jacquard of France, it was possible through it to obtain by machine, elaborate quilted effects closely resembling the lovely designs lavished on the white quilts. Today these Marseilles spreads are prized by collectors.

As we think back to the period when so much effort and time were given to the art of "running fine stitches with a needle," we agree that "good quilters demanded steady nerves, a pleasant temperament, equal dexterity with either hand, an inborn sense of line and form, Job's patience and time galore."[9]

IX
Collecting Quilts

"What should I look for in a quilt?" "What constitutes a *good* quilt?"

With the overwhelming revival of interest in quilts sweeping the country, these become broad questions. In our predicament, we parody an old nursery rhyme,

> Some like them new—some like them old,
> Some want them fresh, but a hundred years old.

In general, the answer is personal taste.

If you want an old quilt, then try to find one with special appeal to you—of historic interest, if you like history. Or, if you are a lover of flowers and gardens, you might look for an old-fashioned floral design that gives pleasure—whether gay and bright or subdued and subtle. If you thrill to the contemporary, look for a quilt that transmits to you the excitement of an abstract painting, either in the crazy design or an adroitly arranged pieced pattern.

Perhaps you want an old quilt because you wish it to fit in with antique surroundings, and you may feel that an eighteenth- or nineteenth-century design in appliqué "belongs" on an imposing four-poster, or that it should be a simple nine-patch to look right on your spool bed. There is no set rule that applies here. As has been pointed out in this book, one of the wonderful aspects of American patchwork quilts is that they seem to fit in with any decor (even modern). A basic Log Cabin can add charm to a four-poster while an appliquéd design can give a spectacular burst of glory to the early American background.

But here is an important consideration. If the quilt is to receive hard usage, don't expect an antique quilt to have the same durability as one composed of new, strong-fibered fabric. To buy a good copy of a fine old design would avoid disappointments.

The choice is yours, and only you can know what you are looking for, just as a bride must make her own choice of china and silver. But remember that a "good quilt" is one that is satisfying to oneself and fits into one's life-style.

If you are collecting quilts for the sake of collecting, and/or as an investment, this is a different story. Naturally today, antique quilts are at a premium, and of course, the better their condition, the greater their market value. In examining an old quilt observe carefully how much it has been mended. Here it should be stated that there are two schools of thought and two questions—to mend or not to mend? One school, and this includes many museums, believes in mending, probably because it helps to preserve any trea-

sure. In the case of quilts, however, it must be judi-
cious mending that retains the old when possible
through expert needlework (darning in particular),
rather than replacing worn-out bits with new materials. The other school of purists prefers to see holes
rather than inserted replacements.

You may hear the question, "How does it happen
that many old quilts are so well preserved, some, in
fact, appearing not to have been used at all?" The
answer is simply stated in a recent article: "Most
women made more quilts in a lifetime than they could
ever use."[1]

True as this may be, a word of warning to the collector of old quilts was sounded in a recent article by
Marvin D. Schwartz,[2] "Remember that quiltmaking
is popular today and many 'bargains' are of recent
vintage." And Cile Blackwood, another antique expert,
advises, "Find a reliable dealer instead of going to
the corner antique shop."

For the enthusiast looking for contemporary quilts
there are groups and individuals producing excellent
copies both in antique designs and original and exciting creations that would please almost any taste. In
fact, there are those who will make quilts on order
to suit individual requirements. Also there are shops
too numerous to list which handle such products.

"Where should I look for quilts?" This is another
not-easy-to-answer question. The quick answer is
"Wherever you can find them." There have never been
so many places making, selling, and advertising quilts
for sale—old and new quilts are everywhere! "But—
is there no place other than commercial outlets where
I can pick them up?"

Actually the situation is no different from collect-

Collecting Quilts

ing antiques of any kind. The same rules apply to the collecting of quilts. The first maxim is: Do not spurn any possible source. Keep both eyes and ears open—things can turn up in the strangest places!

Even the town dump, that popular social place of modern suburbia, can yield pure gold. It has been said, "One man's castoff is another man's treasure." A friend of mine, living in an affluent New England community, a faithful visitor to her "dump," was amply rewarded one Sunday morning when she spotted an old trunk, bursting at the seams, spilling contents that would have tempted even a most uncurious visitor. Two station-wagon loads of loot were salvaged, including twelve exquisite christening robes of various vintages—and what was more exciting, two antique quilts!

Church rummage sales, secondhand stores, thrift shops, and country auctions continue to be favorite gathering places for the hopeful buyer. But prices are high for it seems there is no place remote enough to have escaped an awareness of increased values.

Inquire here and there, especially among friends who are *not* interested in acquiring for themselves, but who might know of someone else's experiences and give you a clue.

It pays to advertise. One lady who has become an avid and discriminating collector of quilts put a small ad in a newspaper: "Patchwork quilts and woven coverlets wanted for personal collection." Those two lines brought a handsome result—the gorgeous Overall Star or Star of Bethlehem quilt made in 1839 (Plate 6).

Experience, of course, is the best teacher in judging

the age of a quilt. Without firsthand information (which is seldom forthcoming) one can never afford to be too careful. A knowledge of materials and dyes is always valuable. Magazines and newspaper articles, filled with helpful material, are being published almost daily, and there are many good books giving standard information. One point that constitutes an element of authority is the homespun and home-woven cloth contained in many old quilts (usually in the lining or backing). There are students of weaving well versed in identifying periods of time through the length and width of the yardage. One knowledgeable lady in the Appalachian region said, "I've spun many a yard—thread-spun, reeled and twisted it—one hundred forty-four threads make a cut—four cuts make a yard."

Exact dates are difficult to establish. While silk, brocade, and velvet materials in a silk quilt may represent different eras, the pieces might have been saved for years and put together at a later date. When some early cotton quilts are held to the light, cotton-seeds may be detected, but this is not infallible proof that the quilt antedates Eli Whitney's patenting of his cotton gin in 1794. Many American housewives continued to use the unprocessed cotton they had on hand right through the latter half of the 1800's.

If paper cut from old dated letters or periodicals was used for backing or foundation, it is possible to indicate a relative date of the quilt (Plates 38 and 39).

An old quilt in my collection is lined with flour sacks, but it took more than knowing the period of the weave of the bags or the date of the brand of the flour to determine when the quilt was actually made.

Collecting Quilts

Proof came through an old document, recounting that the quilt top had been laid away for years before the completion of the quilt.

Just as it takes time, effort, and experience to collect anything worth collecting, so it is with quilts. Visit and study quilt collections at museums throughout the country. Museums are featuring anew American quilts, often upon demand, as visitors ask to see them.

In the New England area, the Shelburne Museum in Shelburne, Vermont, is renowned for one of the finest and most extensive collections of American pieced work and appliqué in the world, and it is beautifully displayed. Beauport, a unique museum by the sea, in Gloucester, Massachusetts, does not display an extensive collection of quilts. But, this "most fascinating house in America" with its fifty-seven rooms, sponsored by the Society for the Preservation of New England Antiquities, is a good example of how quilts can fit into any variety of backgrounds.[3] Here one runs the gamut of quiltmaking amid antiques in their appropriate surroundings. In the Indian Room, the slender-posted early American officers' pine field beds are fittingly dressed with primitive "hit and miss" patchwork quilts, while appropriately near is a rare handmade quilt table, equipped with compartments for quilt scraps and the ever-ready candle in its holder. In a bedchamber called the Byron Room, an early nineteenth-century silk quilt in a star design graces Lord Byron's own mahogany sleigh bed with its ornamentation of carved dolphins.

"What is a quilt worth?" "What should I pay?" "Is

it possible today to collect in a modest way?" The questions pour in from all sides and when it comes to actual market-value prices, these are the hardest of all to answer.

During the years before the revival of interest in quilts the question "What is my quilt worth?" was a usual one, as people wished to dispose of an heirloom quilt, hoping to realize something in the way of cash.

They came to me largely because I was the only person they knew who was at all interested. A truthful answer could have been given quickly, "Only what a buyer will pay—if you have a buyer." Actually, no one (or practically no one) attached any value to an old quilt!

I tried, however, to soften the facts, saying that it was impossible to place a value in dollars and cents on the loving work that had gone into the sewing of those myriads of tiny pieces and the miles and miles of stitches. Oftentimes I looked upon their quilt with longing. But my store of quilts already outweighed a reasonable storage space, and I felt I must be cautious in adding "just one more quilt." Also I hesitated to offer what I felt I should pay. It seemed almost a desecration. The result was that I lost out on many a treasure, only to hear later that a buyer came forth, and the quilt had been picked up by someone who had no qualms in offering less than the figure I had in mind.

Today the situation is in reverse—the market is limited to the extent that the supply will hardly meet the demand. One collector I know well haunts the auctions and thinks nothing of paying three hundred dollars, but he knows his quilts, and a three-hundred-dollar quilt must have some distinction in workmanship or some special feature to attract him. He figures, in this day of rising prices, it may soon be worth one thousand dollars.

Recently at one of the leading New York auction houses a quilt went for nine hundred and sixty dollars. It is now rumored the European prices for American quilts exceed those in America.

The best advice to a neophyte collector is to study carefully before plunging and to know your subject as well as your mind.

X
Caring for Quilts

The cleaning and care of a quilt, old or new, depends upon its condition. Very old quilts that have been packed away for years or handled with extreme care may be as strong in fiber as new ones and can be treated in the same manner.

One learns through experience, but caution is wise. I have seen a beautifully made quilt (top and lining of cotton) in a deplorable state of ruin because the owner did not tell the cleaner it contained an interlining of wool. Quilts composed of strong cotton materials and of fast colors—top, lining, and interlining —may be washed in a home washing machine with satisfactory results. (Recently I was advised by the manager of a reliable laundry to wash my quilt at home as his machines were designed to handle heavier loads and had a stronger action.)

Washing in cold or cool water is safest, using a mild washing powder. If in doubt about the strength

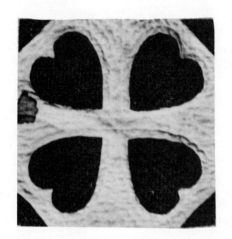

of the cloth, I suggest that you leave it in the washer for only a short span of the full cycle and perhaps not use the dryer. Any quilts with a cotton batting interlining or with the more modern Dacron-polyester filling become soft and fluffy when dried out-of-doors with the air circulating through them. An old-fashioned clothesline is perfect for this and an occasional shaking from time to time is helpful. Little or no pressing is needed. Perhaps pressing the bound edges of a cotton quilt might give it a finishing touch, but in the case of synthetics, *never* press.

In regard to washing modern cotton quilts made with Dacron interlinings, there are widely conflicting views. (I have not had personal experience with these. My quilts are of the cotton batting era.) One very reliable quiltmaking group states that many of their quilt tops and linings are composed of polyester, and that they use Dacron for all their interlinings and have no qualms about washing them by hand and drip-drying. However, they too stipulate *no pressing*. But word comes from a nationally prominent group creating fine quilts of cotton using almost exclusively Dacron interlinings that "we always recommend *dry cleaning* and *no* ironing or pressing."

For quilts made of sateen, dry cleaning is a MUST to retain the sheen and hold the color. This is true also of quilts that contain pieces of glazed fabrics (copperplate, polished calico, and chintzes). If, however, a quilt is of the "plain quilt" type, that is, covered entirely with glazed material, and loses its sheen, there are some dry cleaners who employ a reglazing process.

A majority of old quilts suffer from "brown spots,"

the result of age. If you acquire an old quilt in the hope that such spots will come out in cleaning, be prepared to be disappointed. Chemicals should *never* be used.

The care of old quilts composed of silks, velvets, and brocades (which, of course, cannot be washed) presents a problem all its own. While the brocades and velvets might stand dry cleaning, the silks and satins, in all probability, go to pieces, especially the blacks. If you want to keep the quilt, be satisfied with a good airing and gentle brushing with a soft brush.

As has been stated in the chapter on Collecting Quilts, there are two schools of thought relative to the repairing or maintaining of antique quilts; to repair the worn parts or to replace them with new material which matches as nearly as possible. Just as there are those lovers of antique furniture who believe it detracts from the value of an antique chair to replace its broken leg and/or refinish it, there are others who feel they cannot live with beloved antiques unless they are thoroughly repaired and in usable condition. So it is with quilts, and this problem must be left to the judgment of the owner. (But I have seen quilts badly deteriorated because they had not been properly *cleaned*, aired, and mended.)

For the serious collector who does not plan to use his quilts for practical purposes, careful mending is often his only alternative in order to avoid further depreciation. But for the collector who wishes to use his quilts or display them for his own enjoyment, replacement of worn pieces is his prerogative.

Fortunately for those who need help in rejuvenating a quilt, or perhaps finishing one that was started long

PLATE 47

Pineapple Quilt. This charming quilt, made in China for an American bride of 1791, has an unusual background and is also an outstanding example of trapunto work. Now in the Concord Antiquarian Museum in Concord, Massachusetts, the Museum notes read: "This Chinese spread was a wedding present to Deacon William Parkman's daughter, Sophia, from her Uncle Parkman who got it from China for her. She was married to Samuel Dakin in 1791, and was mother of Mrs. Sarah Richardson." The traditional story is that the quilt was laid away for 150 years (reason unknown), which would account for its pristine appearance.

We wonder about the art of quiltmaking in China, but we can only surmise. Was the art taken there by the American wives of sea captains dealing in the China trade, who often accompanied their husbands on their long voyages? Or did it stem from the indigenous knowledge of quilting, employed by the Chinese themselves, evident for many centuries in their padded and quilted clothing? Courtesy of the present owner, Miss Eileen E. Borland, The Concord Antiquarian Museum.

ago, there has come into being a new profession. In almost every locale, scattered about the country, there are groups and individuals who are making careers for themselves, as well as aiding others, in restoring and making quilts.

Mrs. Irene Dodge, Director of the Wenham Historical Association and Museum in Wenham, Massachusetts, reports that she is receiving calls for help. Members who have discovered quilt tops, or a partly finished quilt tucked deep within the recesses of an old trunk or chest, want to know where to go to have them finished or how to finish them themselves.

Surely one needs only to make inquiry to connect with those engaged in such projects. Publicity is being given to groups, individuals, and shops springing up in every region from Appalachia to California, Pennsylvania to Nebraska, New York to New England, Texas to Oklahoma and South Dakota.

Many such groups were started within the churches during the decline of quiltmaking for the art survived within the church, probably more than in any other place. All through the years women in time of need have banded together to make money to paint the church or patch the roof, and usually this was accomplished by making a few dollars on a quilt.

A group in Antrim, New Hampshire, is an example and theirs is a real success story. The Ladies Circle of the Antrim Baptist Church, including about six ladies who had not forgotten the old art and prompted by the usual reason—to raise money—decided to let it be known that they were available. They placed an advertisement in *Yankee Magazine* a few years ago

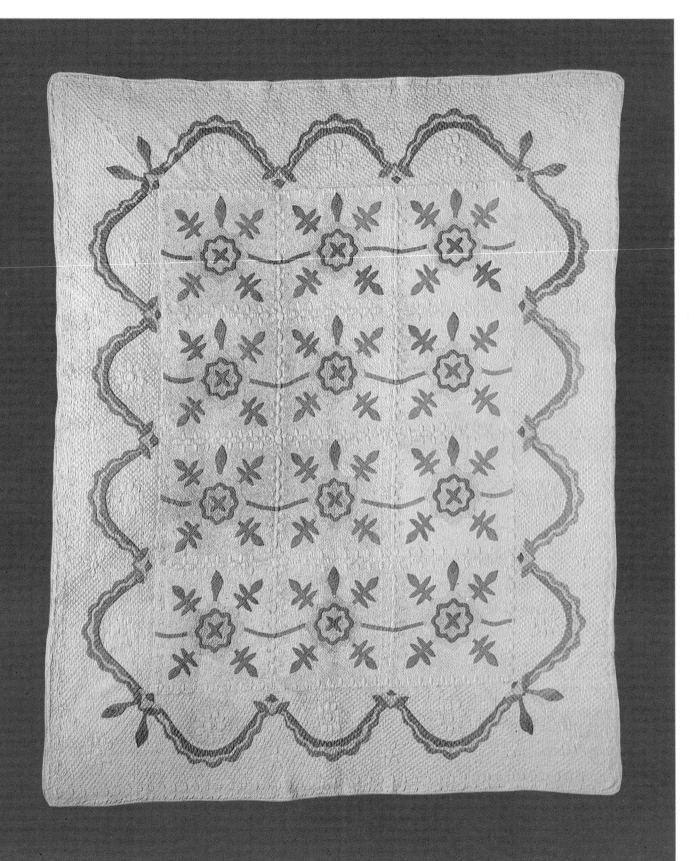

in spite of some strong objections that the expenditure of $4.75 was too much to spend. The ad read:

We make, mend, and quilt quilts.

Responses poured in by the hundreds and the ladies received enough orders to occupy them for several years. Their customers are in more than thirty states including Hawaii, and in foreign countries including Sweden and South America.

The quilting is done at the church on large old-fashioned frames but when I visited the home of Mrs. Carroll Johnson, one of the prime leaders, it appeared that much of the work was centered there. Her rooms overflowed with a colorful mass of quilts in various stages of being created and put together, the small crib quilts light as air and exquisitely quilted in large embroidery hoops. Mrs. Johnson's work is outstanding in creating new designs as well as novel effects in the old patterns. Members of the Ladies Circle continue to be a small group because they frankly say they do not wish to become commercial. "We are a happenstance and we adore our work."

Happily, the mending of old quilts often proves to be less difficult than one might expect, and with a relative amount of skill, one can repair and maintain them oneself.

Bindings often become worn first, and it spruces up a quilt out of all proportion to be given a new one, either in white or a blending color. Bindings cut on the bias of the cloth rather than straight make for a more professional look, conforming more smoothly, especially round the corners. If you know your quilt

PLATE 48

Rose of Sharon. This lovely appliqué design was so often used for that most important of all quilts, the bride's quilt, that it is sometimes known specifically as the Bride's Quilt pattern. Its title, coming from the Song of Solomon, *no doubt appealed to the bride's romantic as well as religious nature. The quilt top for this copy of the old pattern, composed of sateen materials, was made by the author in 1926. The quilting was done by Mrs. Amanda Taylor of Rockwood, Tennessee, one of the few quilters left in that area at that period who could do exquisite work comparable to that of earlier times. The amount of quilting is measured by the number of spools of thread used—here, fifteen spools of one hundred yards each. Bacon Collection.*

Caring for Quilts

is not to receive hard wear, a commercial bias binding is an easy solution. But for greater durability cut your own bias strips one inch to an inch-and-a-quarter in width, to allow for turning in edges.

Replacing worn pieces within your quilt may be a bit tedious, but it is not really a hard task. Sometimes it is impossible to match exactly the color but try to find a material that blends in color and texture. There are charming small-figured calicoes on the market with an old-fashioned look. If the replaced pieces originally had quilting running through them, a small amount of stitches (after the replacement has been made) will do much to make them appear a part of the original design.

In the matter of storing quilts much depends upon the space. Common sense must be the rule, but a few dos and don'ts may prove helpful. An old precaution still holds: Never press cotton quilts before packing them away, to prevent attracting silverfish which eat cotton, and, of course, pressing will yellow the material when stored.

For especially valuable antique quilts, it is suggested that they be rolled on bamboo poles such as are used for carpets, to prevent creasing (which will eventually split). A cover of brown wrapping paper over the whole is advisable to protect from dust. Folding a quilt over and over in the same creases should not be done in any event. This is the most natural thing to do but it accounts for much wear and should be avoided.

In modern life plastic bags seem to be used for everything, and I have read that this is an excellent way to store quilts. This is a misapprehension and can cause yellow streaking and mildew.

Naturally a quilt enthusiast enjoys showing his treasure and while the most effective place to display a quilt is usually on a bed, some quilts are so striking and so beautiful they should be given a place of honor on the wall of one's home as one would hang a fine painting or a subtle tapestry. Perhaps the most satisfactory method is to install a quarter-inch brass rod on the wall where the quilt is to hang—preferably not a wall facing the sun or a strong north light, to avoid fading. A tape or casing is handsewn to the back of the quilt. It should not be machine stitched, as this would detract from the value of the quilt. The casing should be about one-half inch from the top of the quilt to make a slight heading. The rod is slipped through the casing to hold the quilt. This method allows the weight of it to be evenly distributed and prevents wear that would result from sagging if the quilt were hung by rings.

FOOTNOTES

I   Genesis: The Bed and the Quilt

1. Marie D. Webster, *Quilts: Their Story and How to Make Them* (New York: Doubleday Page & Co., 1926), p. 11.
2. Bible, Ezekiel 27: 3, 4, 7.
3. *De Bello Judaics* by Flavius in Webster, *op. cit.*, p. 8.
4. Webster, *op. cit.*, p. 8.
5. Ibid., p. 16.
6. Fred W. Burgess, *Antique Furniture* (New York: G. P. Putnam's Sons, 1919), p. 354.
7. Ibid., p. 354.
8. Ibid., p. 355.
9. Ibid., p. 59.
10. Ibid., p. 408.
11. Ibid., pp. 408, 409.
12. Ibid., p. 409.
13. Webster, *op. cit.*, p. 54.
14. Mary Eden and Richard Carrington, *The Philosophy of the Bed* (London: Hutchinson & Co., Ltd., 1961, republished by Spring Books Brury House, 1966), p. 73.
15. Ibid., p. 73.
16. Ibid. p. 75.

II   Gleanings from Patchwork History

1. Marguerite Ickis, *Standard Book of Quiltmaking and Collecting* (New York: Greystone Press, 1949), p. 256.
2. Marie D. Webster, *Quilts: Their Story and How to Make Them* (New York: Doubleday Page & Co., 1926), p. 41.
3. Ibid., p. 46.
4. Ibid., p. 55.

5. "The Story of the Quilt," *Bulletin*, Public Service Company of Northern Illinois, Vol. 17, No. 10, November, 1948.

6. Webster, *op. cit.*, p. 46.

7. Victoria and Albert Museum, *Notes on Quilting* (London: McCorquodale & Co., Ltd., 1949), p. 5.

8. A. J. B. Wase, *Medieval and Near East Embroideries* (Holton, England: 1935). Quilted padding, a variation of trapunto, is not only used in China today but was worn in medieval times under armor.

9. Webster, *op. cit.*, p. 50.

10. Ibid., p. 50.

11. Victoria and Albert Museum, *op. cit.*, p. 6.

III European Origins of the Quilt

1. Allen H. Eaton, *Handicrafts of the Southern Highlands* (New York: Russell Sage Foundation, 1937), p. 124.

2. Marie D. Webster, *Quilts: Their Story and How to Make Them* (New York: Doubleday Page & Co., 1926), p. 60.

3. *Quilts and Counterpanes in the Newark Museum* (Newark, N.J., 1948), p. 15.

4. Clout meaning patch.

5. From the Massachusetts Historical Society's Collections, quoted in Martha Genung Stearns' *Homespun and Blue* (New York: Charles Scribner's Sons, 1940), p. 8.

6. Quilting was widely used for added warmth in many types of clothing—vests for men, petticoats, a type of hood for children and adults and called "waumus" (warm us), and a snugly fitting garment called "'go-abroady" for ladies to wear under their capes and shawls.

7. Mary Frances Davidson, *The Dye-Pot*, published by the author, Gatlinburg, Tenn. (Printed in the Smokies by Marion R. Mangum, Copyright 1950), p. 1.

8. Ibid., p. 2.

9. Frances Van Arsdale Skinner, author, artist, lecturer and "lover of nature and how to use it."

10. Mary Frances Davidson, *op. cit.*

IV The Quilt in America

1. Victoria and Albert Museum, *Notes on Applied Work and Patchwork* (London: McCorquodale & Co., Ltd., 1949), p. 9.

2. Linsey-woolsey, a textile of wool and linen, or a coarse fabric with cotton warp and woolen filling. The name (for either type) came from Linsey, a village in Suffolk, England, where the material originated.

3. Marie D. Webster, *Quilts: Their Story and How to Make Them* (New York: Doubleday Page & Co., 1926), p. 73.

4. Thomas Hamilton Ormsbee, *Collecting Antiques in America* (New York: Robert M. McBride & Co., 1940), p. 244.
5. Marguerite Ickis, *The Standard Book of Quilt Making and Collecting* (New York: Greystone Press, 1949), p. 47.
6. Martha Genung Stearns, *Homespun and Blue* (New York: Charles Scribner's Sons, 1940), p. 47.

V   Stories About Quilts: Social, Romantic, Political

1. Edith and Harold Holzer, "Patchwork Quilts: Folk Art Relics," *Collector's Weekly*, Vol. 4, No. 158, Sept. 26, 1972.
2. Alice Morse Earle, *Home Life in Colonial Days* (New York: Macmillan Co., 1926).
3. James E. Ayres, "American Coverlets Owned by American Museum in Britain" (Bath, England: Claverton Manor), published first in *Textile History*, Vol. 1, No. 1, December, 1967, p. 7.
4. Harriet Beecher Stowe, *The Minister's Wooing*, quoted in Thomas Hamilton Ormsbee's *Collecting Antiques in America* (New York: Robert M. McBride & Co., 1940), p. 246.
5. Thomas Hamilton Ormsbee, *Collecting Antiques in America* (New York: Robert M. McBride & Co., 1940), p. 246.
6. Ruth E. Finley, *Old Patchwork Quilts and the Women Who Made Them* (Philadelphia: J. B. Lippincott Co., 1929), p. 192.
7. Harriet Beecher Stowe, *The Minister's Wooing*, quoted in Ormsbee, *op. cit.*, p. 246.
8. August C. Buell, *John Paul Jones, Founder of the American Navy*, Vol. I (New York: Charles Scribner's Sons, 1901), p. 244.
9. Buell, *op. cit.*, Vol. II, p. 78.
10. This method of basting the pieces over a paper foundation was employed in the making of many old quilts of silk materials. It was often used in the hexagonal design. See Plates 38 and 39.
11. Martha Genung Stearns, *Homespun and Blue* (New York: Charles Scribner's Sons, 1940), p. 55.
12. Story of the Tree of Life quilt was given to me in 1943 by the late Mrs. Florence Conant Howes, curator of the New England Historic and Genealogical Society, 1934–1958.
13. Miss Stella Jones, *Hawaiian Quilts* (Honolulu, Hawaii: Honolulu Academy of Fine Arts, 1930).
14. James Norman Hall, *Lost Island: Polynesian Island and People*, "Handmade patchwork coverlets which they called tifaifai." A recent authority of South Sea Island dialect states that the correct spelling is tikaikai (meaning sea).
15. Sally McCracken, "Hawaiian Quilts," *Creative Crafts*, No. 27, October, 1972.

VI Victorian Quilt Mania and Decline

1. Copperplate was not a material at all, but a new process of printing cloth in colors, a new method of making chintz and calico.
2. *Bulletin*, Public Service Company of Northern Illinois, Vol. 17, No. 10, November, 1948.
3. Marie D. Webster, *Quilts: Their Story and How to Make Them* (New York: Doubleday Page & Co., 1926), p. 66.
4. Ibid., p. 50.
5. Ibid., p. 51.
6. Florence Peto, *Historic Quilts* (New York: The American Historical Co., Inc., 1939), p. 115.
7. William Rush Dunton, Jr., *Old Quilts*, privately published Catonsville, Md.
8. M. Haehnlen, *Fancy Designs for Ornamental Oriental Work* (Chicago, Ill.: 1884).

VII Renaissance

1. Grace Glueck, "They're Shoo-fly and Crazy, Man," *The New Times*, July 7, 1971.
2. Carol Forbes, "They're Not So Crazy Quilts," *Baltimore Sun*, 1947.
3. Rita Reif, "Quilting is No Longer Just Another Pastime," *The New York Times*, April 25, 1972.
4. S. Robert Pearson, coordinator of *Handcrafts*, 1972.
5. *The Journal of the American Medical Association*, Vol. 215, March 15, 1971.
6. "Craze for Quilts," *Life* magazine, May 5, 1972.
7. "A Passion for Patchwork," *St. Louis Post-Dispatch*, May 9, 1971.
8. *Chattanooga News-Free Press*, Chattanooga, Tenn.
9. *Life* magazine, July 31, 1970.
10. *Look* magazine, August 26, 1970.
11. Edwin A. Roberts, Jr., "Anti-Poverty Success," *National Observer*, June 30, 1969.
12. Mountain Artisans incorporated November, 1968.
13. Exhibit at Greenville County Museum, Greenville, South Carolina, *News*, November 14, 1971.
14. Exhibit at Baltimore Museum of Art, "The Humble Quilt Can Be a Work of Art," *Baltimore Sun Magazine*.
15. Exhibit at Whitney Museum of Art, New York, July–September, 1971. Sixty quilts from more than 300 in the collection of Jonathan Holstein and Gail van der Hoof (pieced quilts of the nineteenth century). Collection exhibited in Paris, France, at the Louvre, summer, 1972.
16. Hilton Kramer, "Quilts Find a Place at Whitney Museum," *The New York Times*, July 3, 1971.

VIII Making Quilts

1. The exhibition "Abstract Designs in American Quilts" held at the Whitney Museum of American Art, July–September, 1971, included quilts: Shoofly, Roman Stripes, Log Cabin, and many others from the collection of Jonathan Holstein and Gail van der Hoof.

2. In reviving the art of appliqué, some imaginative groups of modern patchworkers have brought the art up-to-the-second by using the modern sewing machine, equipped with an attachment enabling them to apply the designs with a stitch called "zigzagging."

3. An exception is the Hawaiian quilt, in which the top consists of one large piece of cloth (often sheets are used as a basis), and the pattern or design which covers the whole has been cut with scissors from another fabric and then applied.

4. In the early days when warmth was the most important thing to be considered, the more humble method of tying knots through the thicknesses was practiced. This method is still used by some quiltmakers. The result is called a "tied quilt." If more interlining is used, the results are puffier and the quilt is referred to as a "comfort" or "comforter."

5. It is interesting that occasionally antique chairs bear the well-defined worn marks on the back slats, showing where a quilt frame has rested.

6. James E. Ayres, *American Coverlets Owned by the American Museum in Britain*, Claverton Manor, Bath, England. (Published first in *Textile History*, Vol. I, No. I, December, 1968), p. 2.

7. A new type of quilting thread is on the market, coated with silicone so it will not tangle or knot.

8. William Rush Dunton, Jr., *Old Quilts* (Catonsville, Md.: Published by the author, 1946), p. 256.

9. Ibid.

IX Collecting Quilts

1. Edith and Harry Holzer, "Patchwork Quilts: Folk Art Relics," *Collector's Weekly*, Sept. 26, 1972.

2. Marvin D. Schwartz, "Antiques: Wide Variety in Early Quilts," *The New York Times*, Feb. 5, 1972.

3. Samuel Chamberlain and Paul Hollister, *Beauport: The Most Fascinating House in America* (New York: Hastings House, 1951).

BIBLIOGRAPHY

Buell, August C. *John Paul Jones, Founder of the American Navy*, Vol. I and II. New York: Charles Scribner's Sons, 1901.

Burgess, Fred W. *Antique Furniture*. New York: G. P. Putnam's Sons, 1919.

Carrington, Eden and Richard. *The Philosophy of the Bed*. London: Hutchinson Co. Ltd. 1961; republished by Springs Books, Drury House, 1966.

Carlisle, Lilian Baker. *Pieced Work and Appliqué Quilts at the Shelburne Museum*. Published by the Shelburne Museum, Shelburne, Vt., 1957.

Clark's N T J & P Coats Book 3 S-22.

Davidson, Mary Frances. *The Dye-Pot*. Privately printed, Gatlinburg, Tenn.

Dunton, William Rush. *Old Quilts*. Privately printed, Catonsville, Md., **1946.**

Earle, Alice Morse. *Home Life in Colonial Days*. New York: Macmillan Co., 1926.

Eaton, Allen H. *Handicrafts of the Southern Highlands*. New York: Russell Sage Foundation, 1937.

Finley, Ruth E. *Old Patchwork Quilts and the Women Who Made Them*. Philadelphia: J. B. Lippincott Co., 1929.

Hake, Elizabeth. *English Quilts Old and New*.

Hall, Carrie E., and Kretsinger, Rose G. *The Romance of the Patchwork Quilt in America*. Caldwell, Idaho: Caxton Printers, Ltd., 1935.

Hall, James Norman. *Lost Island: Polynesian Island and People*.

Ickis, Marguerite. *Standard Book of Quilt Making and Collecting*. New York: Greystone Press, 1949.

McKim, Ruby Short. *One Hundred and One Patchwork Patterns*. Independence, Mo.: McKim Studios, 1931.

McElwain, Mary A. *The Romance of the Village Quilts.* Walworth, Wis.: 1936.

———. *Notes on Applied Work and Patchwork.* London: Victoria and Albert Museum, 1949.

———. *Notes on Quilting.* London: Victoria and Albert Museum, 1932.

Ormsbee, Thomas Hamilton. *Collecting Antiques in America.* New York: Robert M. McBride Co., 1940.

Peto, Florence. *Historic Quilts.* New York: American Historical Society, 1939.

———. *Quilts and Counterpanes in the Newark Museum.* Newark, N.J.: 1948.

Stearns, Martha G. *Homespun and Blue.* New York: Charles Scribner's Sons, 1940.

Webster, Marie D. *Quilts: Their Story and How to Make Them.* New York: Doubleday Page & Co., 1926.

INDEX